COCONUT OIL
NATURE'S PERFECT INGREDIENT

OVER 100 RECIPES INCLUDING HEALTHY DISHES
AND BAKED TREATS TO NURTURE YOUR BODY AND
BEAUTY IDEAS TO FEED YOUR SKIN

LUCY BEE

quadrille

Photography by Ria Osborne

PUBLISHING DIRECTOR Sarah Lavelle
COMMISSIONING EDITOR Lisa Pendreigh
COPY EDITOR Sally Somers
CREATIVE DIRECTOR Helen Lewis
ART DIRECTION AND DESIGN Katherine Keeble
ASSISTANT DESIGNER Emily Lapworth
PHOTOGRAPHER Ria Osborne
FOOD STYLIST Emily Jonzen
PROPS STYLIST Holly Bruce
PRODUCTION DIRECTOR Vincent Smith
PRODUCTION CONTROLLER Emily Noto

First published in 2015 by
Quadrille Publishing Limited

Text © 2015 Lucy Bee Ltd
Photography © 2015 Ria Osborne
Design and layout © 2015
Quadrille Publishing Ltd

Quadrille is an imprint of Hardie Grant
www.hardiegrant.com.au

Quadrille Publishing Ltd
Pentagon House
52–54 Southwark Street
London SE1 1UN
www.quadrille.com

Cataloguing in Publication Data: a
catalogue record for this book is available
from the British Library.

ISBN: 978 1 84949 838 8

Printed in China

FSC
www.fsc.org
MIX
Paper from
responsible sources
FSC® C008047

Thank you for picking up my first ever cookbook.
I hope that as you flick through and read this book,
you'll feel inspired by my selection of favorite family
recipes and go-to healthy foods, all chosen to get
everyone's mouths watering.

COCONUT OIL:
NATURE'S PERFECT INGREDIENT

When I first sat down to write this book,
I spent hours trawling through my recipes
so that I could bring you a collection of the
most delicious—yet healthy—foods imaginable.
I've included extra preparation or cooking tips
wherever I can, with key allergy advice for
each recipe. On pages 184 to 189 you will find
an outline of the nutritional and health benefits
of the ingredients I use most often. I hope that,
with this book as a guide and a jar of coconut
oil to hand, you'll be able to transform your
eating regime. However busy your week gets,
with these recipes you'll always be able to find
enough time to eat healthily.

"THE KITCHEN IS THE HEART OF OUR HOME. FOOD IS THERE TO BE ENJOYED."

One of the questions I am always being
asked is how Lucy Bee coconut oil came to
be. Well, the story behind us is quite simple,
really—our approach is all about eating
unprocessed, fresh, organic foods, where
possible. This means our food is as close to
nature as we can make it.

I've spent my life having to scan labels and
check ingredients. I was diagnosed as celiac
when I was just 18 months old, and back then
there were hardly any preprepared gluten-free
foods on the shelves. Right from my diagnosis,
my parents decided that as a family we should
all eat the same food, which meant most of
our food was cooked from scratch. Years later,
we see this as a blessing in disguise because it
means we've always eaten healthy, nutritious
meals. Throughout our healthy journey, our
vegetable garden has proven to be invaluable,
and we're fortunate enough to have a
seemingly endless supply of cage-free organic
eggs from our six chickens.

Along the way, my parents also taught me
how to become a master at adapting recipes.
I learned how to make pretty much anything
gluten-free, while keeping it tasty, nutritious,
and appealing to the eye. The kitchen is the
heart of our home, and I love nothing more

"AS A STABLE FAT, COCONUT OIL DOESN'T CHANGE ITS PROPERTIES WHEN HEATED."

than getting together with friends or family to share stories of our week over a delicious meal. I hope that this book will encourage you to do the same—after all, food is there to be enjoyed.

SO, HOW DID WE DISCOVER THE WONDER THAT IS LUCY BEE COCONUT OIL?

Well, believe it or not, it all began with a humble egg ...

A family friend, Indra, sent some coconut oil and the book *The Coconut Oil Miracle* by Bruce Fife to us, all the way from Hong Kong. Indra had been raving about this incredible oil and, after reading Bruce's book, we soon realized that it was the missing piece in our jigsaw—finally, we'd found a healthy oil for cooking.

But how does the egg fit in, I hear you ask? Well, the first thing my mom ever cooked with our new jar of coconut oil was a fried egg. As she dished us up her little experiment, she waited for one of the family to complain about how our eggs tasted. However, I didn't even notice, and nor did my dad, sister, and brother. And so began our family journey of cooking with coconut oil.

This was back in 2007 when unrefined coconut oil was almost unheard of and even more difficult and expensive to buy than it is now. Undeterred, we were passionate about sharing our newfound wonder cooking product with the world, so my dad set about finding ways of importing quality coconut oil at an affordable price. Eventually, Lucy Bee Ltd. was founded and we began our quest to

source the very best extra virgin, organic, raw coconut oil on the planet.

Coconut oils taste different depending on the raw materials and extraction methods used, as well as the country that the coconut trees are grown in—a bit like wines, really.

We not only wanted our coconut oil be the best for quality, taste, and price, but it also had to be a Fair Trade certified product, too. After all, we thought it was only right that the lives of the farmers and workers who produce our oil should be improved, as generally coconuts are grown in underprivileged areas.

Our choice of oil also had to be as natural as possible to maintain maximum nutritional benefits. So it was (and remains to this day) a very conscious decision that Lucy Bee coconut oil should be Fair Trade, extra-virgin, raw, and organic.

WHY ARE THE FATS IN COCONUT OIL GOOD FOR US?

For this part, I need to put on my science hat, so try not to switch off! As a nation, we're starting to realize more and more that sugars are our enemy in the obesity crisis, not fats. We need fats for fuel and they are crucial for our health, although it's important that we eat the right kinds to really maximize the efficiency of our body.

Coconut oil is a saturated fat, made up of medium-chain fatty acids (MCFAs). All fats are made up of chains, and the length of the chain just determines how the body breaks it down and uses it. The body deals with medium-chain saturated fats incredibly efficiently, and there's a wealth of research to show just how easily MCFAs are digested, metabolized, and converted to ketones. Coconut oil also happens to be rich in lauric acid (in fact, it's around 48% lauric acid), also found in breast milk and full of health-boosting qualities. It gets turned into monolaurin, which is both antiviral and antibacterial. Finally, as a stable fat, coconut oil doesn't change its properties when heated, which makes it perfect for frying or roasting foods.

So, now you've heard all the good stuff, where do you start? And how much coconut oil should you be eating? Well, there isn't a set amount that you should eat each day, although I would say to aim for between 1 and 3 Tbsp used to replace existing processed oils—as with everything in life, balance is the key.

WHAT EXACTLY IS COCONUT OIL?

It may seem obvious, but coconut oil is extracted from coconut flesh, which is known as the coconut kernel. However, there are different types of coconut oil—refined and unrefined—and it's worth knowing the difference if, like me, you prefer to eat natural foods.

Refined coconut oil will be heavily processed, although it makes up about 90% of the coconut oil on the world market. Unrefined oils, like our Lucy Bee, are natural, unprocessed, and extracted from a more expensive raw material.

The processed version has to be heavily refined to make it fit for human consumption. The oil gets taken from dried copra, which is then turned into crude coconut oil—a completely different oil to virgin or extra-virgin coconut oil. Often, coconuts used for copra will be split in the field with an axe and chunks of coconut flesh collected and taken to a dryer. The dryer can range from solar or even a sophisticated kiln, to a simple rack over a smoky fire. Next, the copra gets bagged up, although by the time it reaches a large-scale industrial oil-seed mill (sometimes overseas and taking months) it is often rancid and moldy. The oil that's extracted from this is a brown color, so it is bleached white as well as deodorized.

"THE COCONUT TASTE OF THE OIL TENDS TO GET LOST WHEN YOU COOK WITH IT."

The virgin or extra-virgin coconut oil process couldn't be more different. It is extracted from the flesh of fresh, mature coconuts within 1 to 4 hours of the coconut being opened and is naturally white in color. It also has a distinctly coconutty aroma and taste, although this differs depending on the country it comes from and how the oil has been extracted:

✦ Cold-pressed extraction is where the oil is extracted from the dried flesh. Our oil from the Solomon Islands and the Dominican Republic are cold pressed by hand.

✦ Centrifuge extraction is where the flesh is first made into coconut milk and the oil is separated from this in a centrifuge.

When I first started using coconut oil, I didn't really notice the difference in taste. Yet, the more I ate—and I eat a lot—the more I became aware of the huge variations. Some oils are quite subtle, whereas others have a more pronounced flavor. What I always find amazing

"WE BELIEVE IN ORGANIC FARMING AND EATING FOODS AS CLOSE TO NATURE AS POSSIBLE."

is that the coconut taste tends to get lost when you cook with it. This means that coconut oil newbies can stop worrying—you shouldn't end up with a coconut-flavored version of all your favorite foods! As much as I go nuts for coconuts, even I wouldn't want that.

The next step after extraction is to package up the coconut oil to be sold in grocery and health food stores across the world. The oils will be solid at temperatures below 75°F (24°C), so in cooler climates, it's solid for most of the year, and in hot countries, such as the Philippines, it is sold as liquid. However, the nutrients and health benefits in the oils are not affected by melting and solidifying.

LUCY BEE EXTRA-VIRGIN FAIR TRADE ORGANIC RAW COCONUT OIL

We had great fun taking our time as we tried and tested oils from all over the world. During our quest, we came across oils that we just didn't like at all. However great the companies were to deal with, if it wasn't right, it had to be: "No, not that one." You see, we only wanted to bring you the very best, and this led us to our first coconut oil, which comes from the Philippines. I think our oil has a delicious and delicate coconut flavor. As well as taste and aroma, we had a few other boxes to tick— things that, for us, were a must-have for our oils. Our jars of Lucy Bee had to be:

✦ **Organic:** We firmly believe in organic farming and in eating foods as close to

nature as possible. This also packs in extra nutritional value, so organic was, for us at least, a no-brainer!

✦ **Extra-virgin:** When you're looking at coconut oil, virgin and extra-virgin mean the same thing. It basically means that the oil is unrefined and unprocessed, which is crucial to our brand.

✦ **Raw:** This means that very little heat has been used during the extraction process—it will go no higher than 32°F (45°C). As raw foodies will tell you, this means that it retains its maximum nutritional benefits.

✦ **Fair Trade:** While the oil is the same whether it's Fair Trade certified or not, being Fair Trade certified lay at the very foundation of our company. We're passionate about making a difference to the lives of our producers, including the workers, the farmers, their families—everyone!

✦ **Glass jars:** Have you ever seen those haunting images of whales washed up on the beach, their stomachs stuffed with plastic? Our horror at seeing those forced us to question the amount of plastic that had wormed its way into our lives. And on top of that are the health implications of plastic toxins leaching into the oil. So we insist on using recyclable glass jars to package and store our oil. The jars are easy to reuse or recycle, which is much better for the environment.

To make it even easier to reuse your jars, we've even come up with an easy-peel label. In the office, we're always competing with one another, coming up with new ideas on how to reuse the jars—our pantry at home is full of Lucy Bee jars holding green tea, homemade spices, and pasta. My mom is a dab hand at finding uses for them, and they can even be used as flower vases or candleholders!

But back to the coconut oil itself. It's important to remember that whatever the country of origin, Lucy Bee is always raw and cold-press extracted from fresh, mature, organically grown coconuts.

If I'm honest, when I was at school and was taught about Fair Trade, I didn't quite get it. I understood about the workers being paid more, of course, but had no idea of the true impact or importance of this. I genuinely didn't know that choosing a Fair Trade certified product could really make such a difference to someone's life. We pay an additional 10% to have Fair Trade oil. Of this, 70% is used for higher wages and 30% for sustainable community projects. Lucy Bee then pays 0.75% of turnover to our Fair Trade certifier, Fair Trade Sustainability Alliance (FairTSA), to help them fund their good works. In the words of Winfried Fuchshofen, FairTSA Director: "We will all continue our path to supporting a fairer world for all, creating new possibilities and living conditions for rural communities around the globe."

Since we launched, Lucy Bee's Fair Trade premium has helped to pay for two wells in the Philippines to bring clean, fresh water to rural villages. Before this, the women had to trek for two miles to fetch water, so you can imagine the difference that this has made to their everyday lives. Thanks to you, our customers, we've also helped to buy solar lightbulbs for the villagers' small, one-roomed wooden homes, and we've even funded scholarships for education. Over in the Solomon Islands, our Fair Trade contributions have paid for everyday benefits, such as medicine and education and here, too, solar bulbs have replaced dangerous kerosene lamps. In the Dominican Republic, our Fair Trade contributions help provide work for abandoned single mothers. They make a huge difference to the lives of individuals and whole villages.

Seeing all this happen in the first couple of years was a real eye opener. It's an amazing feeling to know that when you are buying Lucy Bee coconut oil, you are not only changing your lifestyle into a healthier one, but also improving someone else's life, somewhere in the world. A great feeling, right?

And knowing about Fair Trade has encouraged me to always look for the logo on goods when I'm shopping—bananas, chocolate, coffee, and everything I can. Sometimes these foods may cost a few extra cents, but it's really worth it when you think about the lives they'll change. I have also been encouraged to consider where our food comes from. As well as looking at ingredients, it's good to support local producers and farmers' markets wherever possible. For me, the quality of ingredients, the packaging, production methods, and the ethics behind a food are every bit as important as the taste.

"WHEN BUYING LUCY BEE COCONUT OIL, YOU'RE NOT ONLY CHANGING YOUR LIFESTYLE TO A HEALTHIER ONE, BUT ALSO IMPROVING SOMEONE ELSE'S LIFE."

So, you've bought the book and got your jar of Lucy Bee, but what can you actually do with it? Well, I bet that in no time at all you'll be as hooked as I am on this one, versatile jar of what I like to call "the miracle oil." However, you'll probably mostly use our Lucy Bee as a fantastic, natural oil, or a replacement for processed vegetable oils and butter.

COOKING WITH COCONUT OIL

It's perfect for frying foods such as eggs, onions, garlic, meats, or fish, and, honestly, you only need to use a teeny amount. I don't know why, but a little most definitely goes a long way. Lucy Bee is ideal for roasting, too. You can smear it over meats or fish and toss your vegetables in it, all with wonderful results. If you like the sound of this, then you should definitely check out our recipe for Roast Potatoes page 118—a real winner in our house on Sundays.

You'll also be able to use coconut oil as a replacement for butter in baking, which is great news if you are lactose intolerant. Because Lucy Bee seems to go farther, I find using 25% less than the recommend amount of butter called for in a recipe works just fine. It also has a special kind of sweetness that means you will be able to cut down on the sugar in the recipe by a third, making your cakes instantly healthier! Amazingly though, savory recipes won't be made to taste sweet —instead, the coconut oil simply enhances the flavors, and the coconut flavor is often lost when you cook with it. You can use Lucy Bee as a spread instead of butter, which tastes great on rice cakes or toast. If you decide to try this there is definitely a hint of a coconut

taste, but it works well with jams, yeast extract, or nut butters.

Our wonderful followers on social media also introduced me to Bulletproof coffee (see page 43), which is espresso whizzed with Lucy Bee and grass-fed butter. If you haven't tried this, you must give it a go! It's the ultimate homemade latte and tastes utterly delicious. Whenever somebody new tries it, they can't

"WHEREVER YOU WOULD USE OIL OR BUTTER IN COOKING, GO AHEAD AND SUBSTITUTE WITH LUCY BEE."

get their head around the fact that it hasn't got any milk in it.

You could also try adding a teaspoon of Lucy Bee to smoothies for extra nourishment, and I even stir a teaspoon into my daily cup of green tea—it tastes just perfect, and if you're not a fan of green tea, adding Lucy Bee makes it taste so much better. Plus, it leaves your lips feeling supersoft. How often do you get a drink and lip balm all in one?

While that may seem a whole lot of uses for just one jar, I guess that the simple answer to "How do you use coconut oil?" is this: wherever you would use an oil or butter in cooking, just go ahead and substitute with Lucy Bee.

"I FEEL SO MUCH BETTER WHEN I EAT THE MOST NATURAL, NOURISHING INGREDIENTS POSSIBLE."

EATING AS NATURE INTENDED

As already mentioned, being celiac meant that I had to grow up studying ingredients in all food products, but I know that I feel so much better when I eat the most natural, nourishing ingredients possible. In each of the recipes you read in this book, I recommend that you use organic, unprocessed ingredients—the foods that nature intended—wherever you can. I also prefer to use good-quality, grass-fed meats as I believe not only in the ethos that "we are what we eat," but that "we are whatever we eat has eaten!"

People often ask me if I use other oils, and the answer is yes! As much as I love using Lucy Bee, there's still a place in my pantry for good-quality extra-virgin olive oil to whip up delicious dressings. I also especially like Udo's oil, as a fabulous source of healthy oils.

Because of my intolerance to gluten, my recipes are always gluten-free, but please don't feel you have to do the same.

GROW YOUR OWN

At home, we've always been fortunate enough to enjoy fruit and vegetables fresh from the backyard. Growing up, my siblings and I would roll our eyes and say, "Not again!" as Mom and Dad would serve up delicious meals, telling us with each mouthful how the potatoes or onions were "from the backyard."

It's only now I'm older (and maybe a little wiser!) that I can understand their pride. I love hearing what's growing in our backyard, and knowing that the foods I'll be eating are organic and homegrown—perfect.

Growing your own vegetables is incredibly rewarding, so if you haven't tried it already, why not have a go? You don't need to be

particularly green-fingered and could just start with something easy like sprouting beans and seeds, which taste divine in salads and have incredible health benefits. You could also try some herbs, maybe, and then have fun using them in recipes. It's such an amazing feeling to cook with something that you've grown yourself.

Where possible, I also try to eat foods that are in season. At home we freeze the fruit and vegetables we have an abundance of, to enjoy later in the year. We freeze fruits such as raspberries and blackberries to make wonderful bases for crumbles or coulis, and tomato gluts can be turned into delicious sauces to store in the freezer. My parents even freeze herbs, such as parsley, ready to add to soups and broths.

The other thing that's great about having a vegetable garden is that you can have your own compost heap—an ideal way of using up trimmings, peelings, and leftovers, and great for fertilizing.

KEEPING CHICKENS

Since our journey of using coconut oil began with a humble egg, I guess it's appropriate to mention that this same egg came from one of our own chickens. Nelson, Pepper, Saffi, Sylvia, Doris, and Maggie are never happier than wandering through the vegetable garden, pecking away at their daily treat of Lucy Bee mixed in with their food. They produce the best eggs for us and, hand on heart, I can honestly say that there's nothing better than our own happy chickens' eggs cooked in Lucy Bee. I must thank them for supplying us with delicious food to enjoy every single day.

IT'S ALL ABOUT BALANCE, PLANNING, AND PREPARATION

I really hope that you have fun trying out these recipes and, if you're anything like me, sharing them with your family and friends. There are few better times than a family dinner where we all catch up with what's been going on. Eating healthily is all about balance, and the same can be said about using Lucy Bee in your cooking—everything in moderation.

As you'll see in the recipes in this book, I love trying to turn unhealthy foods into healthy ones by adapting recipes with a Lucy Bee twist. My followers on social media will also know that there are times when I enjoy letting loose and indulging in particular foods. This is where adapting recipes really comes into its own, and I'll have a go at transforming pancakes or

"EVERY TIME YOU EAT OR DRINK, YOU'RE EITHER FIGHTING DISEASE OR FEEDING IT."

cakes, making them not only healthy, but also tasty and satisfying.

I'm sure that you don't need me to tell you that planning ahead can make a huge difference to eating well. I tend to make extra, then either freeze meals or use up spare ingredients in other recipes. Leftover sweet potatoes, for instance, are good cold in a salad, or warm in an omelet the next day—it's always a bonus to open the refrigerator and find leftovers that you can quickly use in another creation!

Before I leave you to read on, I thought I'd share one of my favorite quotes that pretty much sums up my philosophy for life: "Every time you eat or drink, you're either fighting disease or feeding it."

Happy cooking,

ALLERGY INFORMATION

If, like me, you have a particular food intolerance then you will be forever checking packaging and labels to decipher what you can and can't eat. To make your cooking choices easier, each of the recipes in this book is accompanied by a symbol—or symbols—denoting the suitability of the dish for people following specific diets. Below is an at-a-glance guide to what each of those symbols stands for:

✦ Gluten-free — GF

✦ Lactose-free — LF

✦ Wheat-free — WF

✦ Vegetarian — VEG

✦ Dairy-free — DF

✦ Vegan — V

PANTRY STAPLES

These are my everyday essential foodstuffs—the ingredients I always have stored in the pantry or refrigerator, ready for making simple, nutritious meals.

At home, we always make everything from scratch, whether it's our own sauces or even curry powders, so I've tried to include the basics for these here, too, as they can really transform your meals.

✦ **Lucy Bee coconut oil.** This is your new go-to cooking oil. If you need to soften it to use in cooking or baking, then either melt it in the oven as it preheats, or place the jar in warm water, on a radiator, Aga, or even briefly in the microwave.

✦ **Apple cider vinegar.** I love the raw, organic, unfiltered, and undistilled cloudy version, which still has the "mother of vinegar," or cloudy sediment, that contains most of the health-promoting bacterial properties.

✦ **Avocado.** These green fruits taste wonderful on their own, or use to thicken your smoothies. They're rich in antioxidants and folate, too.

✦ **Bragg Liquid Aminos.** This soy sauce alternative is full of amino acids and so tasty too.

✦ **Cacao.** While you can use unsweetened cocoa powder in recipes, cacao is much better for you as it retains all its nutrients and wonderful antioxidants. It can even send moods soaring. What's not to like?

✦ **Cinnamon.** This natural sweetener is a traditional remedy for digestive problems and tastes great added to your oatmeal.

✦ **Eggs.** Organic, cage-free eggs are worth the extra cost, as you know what the chickens have been fed, meaning it's all free from chemicals. I hate the idea of battery hens too, so I always buy organic chicken, and would rather go without if I can't find organic.

✦ **Green tea.** I always have a cafetière on the go, full of green tea.

✦ **Healthy oils.** As well as my Lucy Bee, I keep a bottle of Udo's oil in the pantry for endless body-loving benefits.

✦ **Himalayan pink salt.** Not all salts are equal! This pretty salt helps to balance the body's pH levels, as well as aiding nutrient absorption.

✦ **Nuts.** Brazils, cashews, walnuts, pecans, and almonds are all brilliantly healthy and versatile. Their oils are especially beneficial.

✦ **Seaweeds.** These are great to throw into meals and cooking as they're high in calcium, can alkalize the body, and can even purify the blood.

✦ **Seeds.** I use all sorts of seeds, from pumpkin to sunflower and chia. Try sprouting alfalfa seeds, so easy to do and wonderfully healthy. They make a lovely topping for dishes or filling in sandwiches.

✦ **Spices.** Keep a range, ideally buying them whole and then grinding them yourself in a nut and seed or even coffee grinder, for fresh and cheaper blends. If you make too much of any spice mix, store any extra in your empty Lucy Bee jars.

ESSENTIAL EQUIPMENT

As well as fully-stocked pantry, a range of equipment makes preparing food easier. My must-haves include:

✦ **Blender**

✦ **Spiralizer.** This handy gadget turns vegetables into long, fine strands that can be eaten in place of pasta, as in my "courgetti" recipe on page 80.

✦ **Thermometer or Thermapen**

✦ **Seed and nut blitzer (or coffee grinder)**

✦ **Cafetière**, for green tea.

✦ **Digital scales**, for easy, accurate measurements, especially of very small quantities.

✦ **Food processor**

✦ **Garlic slicer**, while not completely essential this handy gadget saves time and effort, plus it means your hands don't end up smelling overwhelmingly of garlic. Bonus!

✦ **Juicer**

✦ Good-quality **springform cake pans**, to make it even easier to remove your favorite cakes from the pans.

✦ **Heavy-bottom saucepans.** If possible, it's really worth investing in these as the heat is evenly distributed.

✦ **Steamer.** Steaming retains all the nutrients in vegetables, but if you don't have a steamer, place the vegetables inside a metal colander, pop this on top of a large saucepan or pot, fill the pan with just enough water so that the colander isn't touching it, then bring to a gentle simmer and cover.

✦ **Sugar alternatives.** I love stevia, agave nectar, maple syrup, manuka honey, and coconut sugar, and use them in recipes and baking in place of processed sugars.

✦ **Superfoods, to add to smoothies.** Lucuma, spirulina, maca, and chlorella are my favorites.

✦ **Turmeric.** Not only does this add an amazing depth of color to foods, but it brings with it lots of natural anti-inflammatory properties, too. I love sprinkling it over fried eggs.

✦ **Xanthan gum.** Wonderful for gluten-free cooking.

Of course, those in the know will have heard that the wonders of coconut oil don't just stay in the kitchen: being 100% natural and with nothing added, it makes for a fabulous beauty product, too. Read on to find out how we can transform your beauty regime as well...

BEAUTY WITH COCONUT OIL

At first, a lot of people can't quite get their head around the fact that the same oil you cook with can be used on your hair and skin, too. I guess that it probably does sound odd, or at least until you realize that Lucy Bee is 100% coconut oil, with nothing added—totally pure, totally natural.

As a qualified beauty therapist, I am shocked at just how many chemicals we slather on our skin on any given day. Many beauty products are laden with nasties—

"BEING 100% NATURAL, COCONUT OIL MAKES A FABULOUS BEAUTY PRODUCT."

ingredients that we've never even have heard of—and yet we're only too happy to put them on our skin. Skin is the body's biggest organ, and so whatever you put on your skin will be absorbed into the body. When you think about this, doesn't it make sense to use something natural?

As I studied for my beauty therapy qualification, I learned so much about physiology and anatomy, sitting neatly alongside nutrition in caring for your body from the outside in. Coconut oil is the perfect link to heal the body naturally. This is why Lucy Bee makes such a fabulous beauty product; it has so many uses that I can't even begin to list them all. However, my favorites are as a:

✦ **Moisturizer:** Rich in vitamin E, coconut oil can nourish and moisturize even the driest of skins. In fact, you only need to use a small amount, and then simply massage into your skin. It can help soften the appearance of fine lines and plump up the skin, and it's even suitable for oily skin types too. What makes coconut oil so great as a moisturizer is that you really don't need to add anything else—it works amazingly well just as it is.

✦ **Makeup remover:** This is my all-time favorite beauty use. All you need to do is warm a small amount of oil between your fingertips before massaging over the skin and wiping away with a cotton pad or face cloth. It even removes waterproof mascara and can help to strengthen eyelashes at the same time. What's not to love?

✦ **Cuticle rub:** If I'm cooking and have a little Lucy Bee left over, I use it to rub into my cuticles. It nourishes them, stimulating new nail growth by increasing circulation in the nail bed.

✦ **Deodorant:** I can already sense a few of you are looking a little skeptical, but this really does work. Rub a small amount under your arms and see for yourself.

✦ **Hair conditioner:** At least once a week, I spend a night in and massage Lucy Bee coconut oil into my hair and scalp. I'll then tie my hair up and leave the oil in overnight to condition my hair. You'll need to give it a couple of shampoos to wash it out, but you'll find your hair is softer and shinier than ever before. I've seen a huge difference and try to do this more often. I must admit, I love to straighten and curl my hair, but since using Lucy Bee it's really helped to condition my hair.

✦ **Body scrub:** If you mix Lucy Bee coconut oil with detoxifying Himalayan salt or Epsom salts, it makes the best body scrub ever—the perfect body preparation before your summer vacation or a big event. You can also apply a thin layer of the Lucy Bee "magic" directly onto your body, making it feel amazing once you get out of the shower.

✦ **Massage oil:** Lucy Bee is a fantastic massage oil, even for delicate newborn skin. If you want to make your massage oil into a holistic treatment, add some essential oils to the coconut oil. The essential oil aroma you choose can vary depending on your mood and whether you prefer a detoxifying or relaxing treatment.

✦ **Oil pulling:** This is an ancient Ayurvedic treatment for ridding the body of toxins and for whitening teeth. Place between a teaspoon and tablespoon of Lucy Bee coconut oil in your mouth and wait for it to melt, then swish it about, just like you would mouthwash, for anywhere between five and 20 minutes. Then spit it out into the trash, rather than the sink, to avoid blocking the drain.

✦ **Toothpaste:** Believe me when I say that your teeth will feel superclean and look whiter after using coconut oil toothpaste.

AND IT DOESN'T STOP THERE …
Just as coconut oil is good for us, it's also good for our pets. We've seen this first hand with our chickens, as well as the pheasants and ducks who turn up most days at the back door, waiting for their fix of Lucy Bee, water, and oats. I breakfast most mornings with the ducks, even though I often end up telling them off for fighting over who gets to eat the most oats. Of course, who can blame them when it's covered in Lucy Bee!

Happily, since we love animals, barely a day goes by when we don't hear from one of our followers telling us how their pet has benefited from Lucy Bee too. We've seen photos of Lucy Bee helping every animal from horses and dogs to cats, geckos, and even tortoises.

If that weren't enough, we've even greased garden shears with Lucy Bee, successfully fixed a pair of shoes that wouldn't zip up after one wear (and it's still working fine to this day) and eased a stiff sash window. I told you that Lucy Bee is a versatile and miracle oil!

"COCONUT OIL IS THE PERFECT LINK TO HEAL THE BODY NATURALLY."

BODY SCRUB

1 Tbsp coconut oil
1 Tbsp Himalayan salt or Epsom salts
8 to 12 drops essential oil (choose rose oil for
    calming, eucalyptus for energizing, or
    lemon for detoxing)
Dry body brush

Place the coconut oil, salts, and essential oils
in a ceramic dish and mix until thoroughly
combined. Using a dry body brush, brush the
oil all over your body. Always work the strokes
of the body brush in the direction toward
your heart.

MASSAGE OIL

1 Tbsp coconut oil
6 to 8 drops essential oil or blend (consult a
    practitioner to learn which essential oils
    are best for you)

Place the coconut oil and essential oil or
blend in a ceramic dish and mix until
thoroughly combined.

TOOTHPASTE

1 Tbsp coconut oil, slightly softened
1 Tbsp baking soda
3 drops edible peppermint oil (optional)

Place the coconut oil, baking soda, and edible
peppermint oil, if using, in a ceramic dish and
mix well together. Use as you would a normal
toothpaste.
    Keep this in a small container in the
bathroom. The first couple of times you use
this toothpaste, you will notice it can taste
different from store-bought toothpaste, but
stick with it because you will be pleased with
the results. Baking soda is softer than tooth
enamel so does not damage your teeth.

BREAKFAST & BRUNCH

I'm a granola addict and find it difficult to restrain myself from eating this by the handful—it's simply irresistible! Homemade coconut granola is great at any time of the day, not just for breakfast, as it really boosts my energy levels and sends them soaring. For breakfast, I have a bowlful of granola served with my homemade Almond Milk (see page 182), but this also tastes good on top of crumbles, yogurt, or pancakes —go wild!

COCONUT GRANOLA

¼ cup (60 g) coconut oil, melted
1¼ cups (100 g) gluten-free oats
⅓ cup (50 g) chia seeds
1 tsp ground ginger
1 tsp ground cinnamon
½ cup (50 g) pecans
⅓ cup (30 g) dried shredded coconut
¼ cup (50 g) golden raisins
¼ cup (50 g) big juicy raisins
⅓ cup (40 g) hazelnuts
¼ cup (30 g) pumpkin seeds

SERVES 4

Preheat the oven to 275°F (140°C). Line a baking sheet with parchment paper.

Place all the dry ingredients in a mixing bowl, add the melted coconut oil, and stir well using a wooden spoon, until coated in the oil. Tip onto the prepared sheet, ensuring that the mixture is spread out evenly.

Bake in the oven for 50 minutes, stirring a couple of times to make sure it doesn't stick and burn. Remove from the oven and let cool for 10 minutes. If you want extra-crunchy granola, turn the oven off and leave the door open, with the granola still inside.

VARIATIONS
For extra sweetness, add 1 tsp lucuma powder to the granola mixture. For a chocolate fix, add 2 Tbsp (30 g) cacao nibs.

PREWORKOUT SCRAMBLED EGG

1 tsp coconut oil
½ chile, minced
2 scallions, minced
2 or 3 large eggs, beaten
2 large handfuls of spinach, washed
¼ cup (20 g) crumbled feta

TO SERVE
½ avocado, chopped
Squeeze of lime juice, to taste

SERVES 1

This amazing breakfast fills me with energy for the day ahead. It's full of good fats to really put a spring in your step—nothing else is required, except maybe a Bulletproof Coffee (see page 43)!

Melt the coconut oil in a nonstick saucepan over medium heat and add the chile and scallions. Gently sauté until softened.

Add the beaten eggs to the pan, then throw in the spinach. Stir until it resembles scrambled egg. Stir in the feta, then spoon onto a plate and serve with the avocado and a squeeze of lime.

SWEET POTATO AND FRIED EGG WITH ARUGULA

5 oz (140 g) purple sprouting broccoli
2 tsp coconut oil
Cooked sweet potato, diced
½ tsp dried red pepper flakes,
    or to taste
1 large egg
Himalayan salt and black pepper
Handful of arugula, to serve

SERVES 1

This dish is simply the best, especially when you have leftover sweet potato, as it's superquick, easy, and nutritious. Start your day with the right foods to fuel your body, and you'll soon see a difference.

Steam the sprouting broccoli for about 4 minutes, until softened.

Meanwhile, melt half the coconut oil in a small frying pan over medium heat. Add the sweet potato and pepper flakes and cook until warmed through. Tip onto a plate.

Melt the remaining coconut oil in the pan, crack the egg into it, and fry to your liking, then season. Transfer to the plate along with the steamed broccoli. Add some arugula on the side and serve.

BREAKFAST & BRUNCH

Sometimes—usually the morning after the night before—you need a good fry-up to get you going; these sautéed tomatoes really finish things off a treat. They're the perfect addition to a brunch and are great on a slice of gluten-free toast, topped off with a fried or poached egg. For a fantastically filling and nutritious lunch, serve on a slice of polenta, sprinkled with chopped parsley or chives. Or add to an omelet with pancetta, samphire, and thyme sprigs.

SLOW SAUTÉED TOMATOES

1 to 2 tsp coconut oil
14 oz (400 g) cherry tomatoes
Pinch of dried thyme
Himalayan salt and black pepper

SERVES 2

GF | WF | DF | LF | V

Melt the coconut oil in a heavy-bottom frying pan over low heat.

Add the tomatoes and thyme, and season well with salt and pepper. (Don't skimp, the seasoning really adds flavor and depth to the tomatoes.) Cover and cook for 20 minutes.

Remove the lid and continue cooking for 10 minutes to reduce the liquid. Serve alongside a delicious Lucy Bee-style fry up!

For some reason, smoked salmon always feels like a real treat. It reminds me of brunch on Christmas Day, so having this tasty breakfast midweek or at the weekend really fills me with joy. A drizzle of balsamic vinegar over the top works well.

SCRAMBLED EGG WITH SMOKED SALMON AND AVOCADO

1 large avocado, sliced
6 slices of smoked salmon,
    or to your taste
Lemon juice, to taste
4 large eggs
2 tsp coconut oil
1 Tbsp chopped fresh parsley
Himalayan salt and black pepper

SERVES 2

Arrange half a sliced avocado and three slices of smoked salmon on each plate. Squeeze over lemon juice and sprinkle with salt and pepper to taste.

Crack the eggs into a bowl and season, before lightly beating together.

Melt the coconut oil in a nonstick saucepan over medium heat, then add the eggs and stir continuously until they thicken to your preferred consistency, making sure you don't overcook them or they will turn dry. As they will continue to cook even after you remove them from the heat, take them off the heat just before you think they are ready.

Spoon the scrambled eggs onto the plates, sprinkle over some parsley, and serve immediately.

Breakfast is my favorite meal of the day as it's so important for keeping you healthy and happy, yet so many people seem to skip it. However, there's no excuse to miss breakfast when you can have this filling and nutritious oatmeal before you head off for the day. Choose your own toppings, as pretty much anything goes.

OATMEAL, LUCY BEE STYLE

½ cup (40 g) gluten-free oats
⅞ cup (200 ml) almond milk,
    or water
1 tsp coconut oil

TOPPING SUGGESTIONS
Mix and match toppings,
according to your preference:
• ½ banana, sliced • blueberries
• raspberries • strawberries • goji
berries • hazelnuts • pumpkin seeds
• toasted hemp seeds • 1 tsp ground
cinnamon • 1 tsp nut butter • 1 tsp
manuka honey • 1 tsp cacao nibs
and/or raw chocolate sauce.
If you like protein powders, you can
add these—I use a vegan one, which
I stir into the oatmeal for a boost.

SERVES 1

Put the oats, almond milk or water, and coconut oil in a saucepan and gently bring to a boil. Once it bubbles and the oats have absorbed the liquid, stir well, remove from the heat, and let rest for 3 to 4 minutes.

Pour into a bowl and sprinkle over your chosen topping or toppings.

These savory muffins, which are actually more frittatas than muffins, taste lovely when eaten warm, fresh from the oven, and are just as delicious at room temperature. In our house, they barely make it to the table as everyone fights over them. They make an excellent breakfast on-the-go.

SMOKED HADDOCK AND HORSERADISH MUFFINS

9¾ oz (275 g) smoked haddock
3½ Tbsp (50 ml) milk
1 Tbsp coconut oil
3½ oz (100 g) leeks, finely sliced
1 garlic clove, minced or crushed
4 extra-large eggs
2 tsp horseradish sauce or
    1 tsp fresh grated horseradish
⅛ cup (10 g) grated Parmesan
Himalayan salt and black pepper

SERVES 4 (MAKES 8 MUFFINS)

Preheat the oven to 350°F (180°C). Line a muffin pan with 8 paper muffin liners. Alternatively, grease 8 molds of the pan with a little coconut oil.

Place the smoked haddock in a shallow ovenproof dish, pour over the milk, cover the dish with foil, and cook in the oven for 15 minutes. Drain and set aside until cool enough to handle.

Meanwhile, heat the coconut oil in a heavy-bottom frying pan and add the leeks and garlic. Cover and sauté for 5 minutes until softened, then remove the lid and cook off any liquid.

Beat the eggs with some salt, pepper, and the horseradish sauce or fresh grated horseradish. Flake the haddock into small pieces and stir into the egg mixture.

Spoon the mixture into the muffin liners or pan, then sprinkle the Parmesan over and bake in the oven for 20 to 25 minutes. Let cool for 5 minutes, before transferring to a wire rack. Serve hot or let cool.

This is a good way to start your day, and the ideal breakfast recipe to help you think outside the cereal box. The quinoa will keep you full all morning, and will help those energy levels to soar. I like to serve this with a slice of gluten-free bread to mop up any egg yolk and tomato juices.

QUINOA-STUFFED MUSHROOMS WITH GARLIC TOMATOES AND POACHED EGG

¼ cup (40 g) quinoa
⅞ cup (200 ml) vegetable broth
   or water
8 cherry tomatoes, halved
1 garlic clove, minced
1 Tbsp coconut oil, melted
4 flat mushrooms, ideally Portobello,
   stalks removed
Handful of cashews (optional)
2 large eggs
Handful of baby spinach leaves
Himalayan salt and black pepper

TO SERVE
Chopped fresh parsley or pea shoots
Slices of gluten-free bread

SERVES 2

GF | WF | DF | LF | VEG

Preheat the oven to 350°F (180°C).

Put the quinoa and broth (for more flavor) or water in a pan and cook over medium heat for 10 to 12 minutes, until softened. Drain and set aside.

Place the tomato halves on a baking sheet, sprinkle with the garlic, drizzle over half the coconut oil, and season with salt and pepper. Place the mushrooms and cashews, if using, on a separate baking sheet and brush with the remaining coconut oil, then place both sheets in the oven and bake the tomatoes for 15 minutes and the mushrooms and cashews for 10 minutes.

Stuff the cooked mushrooms with the drained quinoa, then return to the oven for another 5 minutes.

Meanwhile, add boiling water to about a 4-in (10-cm) depth to a pan. Lower the heat so that the water is just off a boil, then crack both eggs into the water and cook for 3 minutes (for a runny yolk). Remove with a slotted spoon.

Spread a layer of spinach across each plate, then add the mushrooms and cashews. Sprinkle the tomatoes over the mushrooms and then place poached egg on top. Season, sprinkle over chopped parsley or pea shoots, then serve immediately with slices of gluten-free bread.

As my followers on social media will know, I have a slight addiction to pancakes, but thankfully my addiction is a healthy one. There are SO many different ways to make pancakes. I like using either quinoa flakes, buckwheat flour (despite the name this is actually a fruit seed and is gluten-free), or oats.

PANCAKES ANYONE?

1 banana
2 eggs
¼ cup (40 g) quinoa flakes
1 tsp ground cinnamon
1 tsp coconut oil

TOPPING SUGGESTIONS
- Walnuts and pumpkin seeds with cinnamon and manuka honey
- Greek yogurt with fruit
- Banana, peanut butter, and cacao nibs
- Salted Chocolate Almond Butter (see page 182)
- Almond milk, cacao, and manuka honey (blended together to make a sauce) with berries
- Lemon juice with coconut sugar
- Greek yogurt with Healthy Seed Mix (see page 182)

SERVES 1

Put the bananas, eggs, quinoa flakes, and cinnamon in a blender and blend together.

Melt the coconut oil in a small frying pan, then pour in the pancake batter in batches to make small pancakes. Fry for 3 minutes on each side until cooked through.

Serve with a selection of toppings, either from the list of suggestions (see left) or your own favorite—the world's your oyster!

OVERNIGHT CHIA AND COCONUT PUDDING WITH SAUTÉED BANANA

⅓ cup (50 g) chia seeds
2 Tbsp (30 ml) coconut yogurt
⅞ cup (200 ml) almond milk
½ tsp ground cinnamon
½ tsp ground nutmeg
1 Tbsp dried shredded coconut
  (optional)
1 tsp manuka honey
1 banana
1 Tbsp coconut oil
1 Tbsp pomegranate seeds

**SERVES 2 GENEROUSLY,
OR 4 SMALL SERVINGS**

So many people fall back on cereals for breakfast, but they're usually laden with sugar and won't keep you full or happy until lunchtime. This is a great alternative breakfast option that will pack your body with healthy fuel for the day ahead. Sleep is a time machine to breakfast—I often go to sleep dreaming of this after making it for the following morning.

Put the chia seeds, coconut yogurt, and almond milk into a small bowl. Stir in the cinnamon, nutmeg, dried shredded coconut, if using, and honey, then pour into two (or four) bowls or glasses and let set in the refrigerator overnight.

When ready to serve, slice the banana about ¾ in (2 cm) thick. Sauté in a frying pan with coconut oil over high heat for 1 to 2 minutes or until caramelized.

Spoon banana slices on top of each chilled pudding and then sprinkle over a handful of pomegranate seeds.

VARIATION
Instead of banana, sauté chopped apple in coconut oil that has been infused with cloves: Heat the oil gently in a pan and add 4 cloves. After a couple of minutes the clove aroma will be released. Remove the cloves from the pan and add the chopped apple to sauté.

BREAKFAST BANANA AND KIWI WITH TOFU AND CHIA SEEDS

4 tsp coconut oil
13½ oz (100 g) ripe banana
6¼ oz (175 g) kiwi, peeled
7 oz (200 g) silken tofu
¼ cup (40 g) chia seeds
½ cup (50 g) cashews

SERVES 2 TO 3

While this may sound like an odd combination, trust me when I say that it tastes phenomenal. The silken tofu is incredibly creamy, which will make this dish feel as though you're eating dessert for breakfast—and that's never a bad way to start the day, right?

Blend all the ingredients together in a food processor until smooth. Let stand for 30 minutes to thicken, then serve in bowls.

GREEN TOFU SMOOTHIE

4 tsp coconut oil
⁷⁄₈ cup (200 ml) coconut water
3½ oz (100 g) silken tofu
1 oz (30 g) spinach, ½ avocado, 1 kiwi,
    peeled, and 1¾ oz (50 g) mango or
    pineapple flesh
1 tsp lucuma powder
1 Tbsp Healthy Seed Mix (see page 182)

When you're running low on time in the morning, this makes a great breakfast on-the-go. Simply blitz it up, pour it into a recycled Lucy Bee jar, and run!

Put all the ingredients in a blender, then blitz to a smooth mixture. Serve immediately, topped with dried shredded coconut, goji berries, or cacao nibs, if desired.

SERVES 1

MANGO LASSI

1 tsp coconut oil
Flesh of 1 mango
7 Tbsp (100 ml) kefir (or plain yogurt)
3½ Tbsp (50 ml) almond milk
1 tsp orange blossom water
1 tsp manuka honey
Seeds of 1 cardamom pod, crushed

Kefir is a cultured milk that is rich in healthy probiotic bacteria, as well as being a good source of B vitamins, minerals, and essential amino acids.

Put all the ingredients in a blender and blitz together until smooth and thick. Serve immediately.

SERVES 1

BLUEBERRY BEE BLITZ

1 tsp coconut oil
⅓ cup (50 g) frozen blueberries
1 small or ½ medium banana
7 Tbsp (100 ml) kefir (or plain yogurt)
3½ Tbsp (50 ml) coconut milk

This smoothie works brilliantly made with frozen blueberries, so always keep your freezer stocked.

Put all the ingredients in a blender and blitz together until smooth and thick. Serve immediately.

SERVES 1

BULLETPROOF COFFEE

3 to 4 tsp coconut oil
1 shot of espresso coffee
3 to 4 tsp grass-fed,
    organic, unsalted butter

SERVES 1

This is the ultimate preworkout drink. Plus, it tastes every bit as creamy as your favorite latte.

Put all the ingredients into a blender and blend until completely combined. This ensures the oil doesn't separate and lie on the top.

LUNCH BITES

Sushi is actually incredibly easy to make and is a really tasty and nutritious lunch or supper. I find that sushi fillings tend to be a really personal thing, so mix and match according to your mood, and it's a great recipe to make with friends so that you can all try out your favorites.

BROWN RICE OR QUINOA SUSHI

Scant 1 cup (170 g) brown rice
or quinoa
Scant 1 cup (225 ml) water
1 Tbsp coconut oil
Dash of rice vinegar
4 to 6 nori sheets

FILLING SUGGESTIONS

- Avocado, sliced
- Smoked salmon, shredded
- Cream cheese
- Red bell pepper, finely sliced
- Cucumber, peeled, seeded, and cut into matchsticks

SERVES 2 TO 4

GF WF

Place the rice or quinoa in a saucepan. Add the water and the coconut oil, with the rice vinegar, if using. Over low heat, gently simmer the rice or quinoa until cooked, adding a little more water if necessary to prevent it from burning. Alternatively, cook the rice or quinoa according to the package directions. Once cooked, set the rice or quinoa aside to cool.

Lay a nori sheet on a lined baking sheet, rough side up. Spread a thin layer of cooked, cooled rice or quinoa evenly over the sheet, leaving a 1-in (2.5-cm) border on the side farthest away from you. Sprinkle over your choice of filling, without overcrowding them.

Pick up the side of the nori sheet closest to you and gently start to roll the sheet, keeping it nice and tight. When you get to the side farthest from you, wet it with your finger to ensure that the nori sticks together. Repeat with the remaining nori sheets, rice, and fillings.

Wet a very sharp knife and cut the rolled sushi into roughly 1-in (2.5-cm) sushi bites, keeping the knife wet in between each cut, and avoiding touching the nori too much with your hands. Each nori sheet will make between 6 to 8 sushi bites.

Serve the sushi on plates with a bowl of soy sauce for dipping as the perfect finger food.

Exotic mushrooms with hard-to-pronounce names are now being grown everywhere, which is good news as they are not only delicious but come with many health benefits too. Varieties such as enoki, shiitake, oyster, and shimeji are becoming more widely available, and are immune-boosting wonders.

CREAMY SAGE POLENTA WITH EXOTIC MUSHROOMS

FOR THE POLENTA
2 cups (500 ml) milk or almond milk
⅞ cup (200 ml) water
1 sprig of sage (about 6 leaves),
    plus extra fried in a little coconut
    oil until crisp, to serve (optional)
½ cup (75 g) instant cornmeal
1 tsp Himalayan salt
1 Tbsp coconut oil, melted
Scant ¼ cup (15 g) grated Parmesan

FOR THE MUSHROOMS
1 Tbsp coconut oil
5¼ oz (150 g) mixed exotic
    mushrooms
Dash of fish sauce
3 oz (80 g) broccoli, cut into small
    florets and steamed
Himalayan salt and black pepper

SERVES 2

Put the milk, water, and sage into a saucepan and bring almost to a boil. Pour in the cornmeal and salt, whisking as you go, and continue to whisk over low heat until the cornmeal is an oatmeal-like consistency, 5 to 7 minutes.

Stir in the melted coconut oil and remove from the heat. Remove the sage and add the Parmesan, stirring with a wooden spoon.

For the mushrooms, heat the coconut oil in large frying pan and add the mushrooms. Sauté for a couple of minutes, adding the fish sauce, until tender. Stir in the steamed broccoli florets and season to taste.

Serve the creamy polenta in shallow bowls with the mushrooms on top, garnished with crispy fried sage leaves, if using.

When I was younger, one of the things I felt I missed out on was chicken nuggets. My Uncle Ash used to make these healthy, gluten-free chicken fingers all the time and they were so tasty that my friends only ever wanted his version of nuggets. Eventually, they became known as AFC (Ash's Favorite Chicken)! These are ideal to serve to friends with dips, with Celeriac Fries (see page 116) or Roasted Sweet Potato Wedges (see page 120), or with a green salad.

CHICKEN FINGERS

3 tsp mild curry powder (or see
  page 181 for homemade)
1 tsp five-spice powder
1 tsp dried tarragon
Pinch of sweet paprika (optional)
14 oz (400 g) skinless chicken fillets
  or chicken breast cut into finger-
  size pieces
2 large eggs, beaten
Scant 2 cups (200 g) gluten-free
  bread crumbs
3½ Tbsp coconut oil

SERVES 2 TO 4

In a medium-large bowl, mix together the curry powder, five-spice, and tarragon, with the paprika, if using, then add the chicken pieces and turn to coat in the mixture. Let stand for 10 to 20 minutes.

Put the beaten eggs and bread crumbs into two separate shallow dishes. Dip each chicken piece first in the egg, then coat in the bread crumbs and place on a plate.

Heat the coconut oil in a heavy-bottom frying pan until hot, then add the chicken and cook for about 4 minutes before turning and cooking for another 4 minutes, depending on thickness. If unsure, check they are cooked using a Thermapen (thermometer).

Sometimes, all you want to do is kick back on the couch and cozy up in front of the TV with your favorite comfort food. However, this pizza will change your life. I mean, what's not to love about turning something bad on its head and making it completely healthy and gluten-free? These are my favorite toppings, but feel free to play around with your own combinations.

CAULIFLOWER PIZZA GF WF

FOR THE BASE

1 medium cauliflower, coarsely chopped
2 eggs, lightly beaten
Scant ¼ cup (20 g) buckwheat flour
2 tsp mixed dried herbs
Pinch of Dukkah Spiced Seed Mix (see page 181) or dried red pepper flakes
1 Tbsp coconut oil, melted
Himalayan salt and black pepper

FOR THE TOMATO SAUCE

1 Tbsp coconut oil
3 large garlic cloves, crushed
14-oz (400-g) can chopped tomatoes
Juice of ½ lemon
1 tsp mixed dried herbs or 3 fresh thyme sprigs (optional)

TOPPING SUGGESTIONS

- Buffalo mozzarella and fresh basil
- Goat cheese and watercress
- Kalamata olives and crumbled feta
- Smoked salmon and arugula (add just before serving)

SERVES 4

Preheat the oven to 350°F (180°C). Line a flat baking sheet (a nonstick pizza baking sheet is ideal) with parchment paper.

Blitz the cauliflower in a food processor until it resembles rice grains. Transfer to a bowl and stir in the beaten eggs, buckwheat flour, herbs, spiced seed mix or red pepper flakes, and some seasoning. Knead the mixture to a doughlike consistency.

Roll out the dough evenly and thinly on the lined sheet, making either one or two bases. A good technique is to spread out the dough, place plastic wrap over the top and, using a rolling pin, roll out. Using a pastry brush, brush the melted coconut oil over each base. Bake in the oven for 25 to 30 minutes, until crispy.

Meanwhile, to make the tomato sauce, melt the coconut oil in a saucepan, add the garlic, and sauté until golden, then add the chopped tomatoes, lemon juice, and herbs. Simmer for 20 minutes uncovered until the sauce almost resembles a paste, taking care as the sauce may stick to the pan.

Spread the tomato sauce over the cooked bases and add your choice of toppings. If the toppings need cooking, cook in the oven for another 15 minutes.

PEPPERS AND TOMATOES WITH ANCHOVIES ON POLENTA

1 Tbsp coconut oil, plus
    extra for frying
1¾-oz (50-g) can anchovies in oil
2 garlic cloves, thinly sliced
¼ lb (600 g) bell peppers, a mixture
    of colors, seeded and thinly sliced
7 oz (200 g) cherry tomatoes
Cooked polenta, cut into pieces
    2 by 1¼ in (5 by 3 cm) (large
    fudge size)
Handful of torn basil or arugula
    leaves, to serve

SERVES 2

I love this Mediterranean-style combination of flavors. Close your eyes and you could almost be lunching in Italy. Any leftovers taste great the next day, on their own or in an omelet.

Put the coconut oil, anchovies, and garlic in a heavy-bottom frying pan over medium heat. Add the peppers and tomatoes, give it a good stir, then cook over medium heat for 15 minutes, until the peppers have softened. Tip into a bowl and keep warm.

    Add a touch more coconut oil to the wiped-out pan and, when hot, add the polenta pieces and fry on each side until golden.

    Place the polenta on a plate, spoon the pepper mixture over, and serve topped with basil or arugula leaves.

POLENTA WITH CHILE

4½ cups (1 liter) water
1¾ cups (250 g) instant cornmeal
2 tsp Himalayan salt
2 tsp ground black pepper
Few shakes of red pepper flakes
1 Tbsp coconut oil

SERVES 6 TO 8

This spiced polenta makes a lovely side dish or addition to salads or roasted vegetables. If you like having something starchy to mop up your dinner, this spiced polenta makes an excellent alternative to sweet or roast potatoes. Delicious!

Place the water in a large saucepan and bring to a boil. Turn the heat down to low and tip in the cornmeal in a steady stream, stirring constantly. Continue stirring as the cornmeal thickens, about 3 minutes.

    Stir in the salt, pepper, red pepper flakes, and coconut oil. Pour the cornmeal into a square or rectangular dish and let set—when ready, it should be firm to the touch.

    When ready to serve, tip the polenta out of the dish and cut into pieces, as required. It will keep for a few days in the refrigerator and also freezes well.

VARIATION
For a cheesy version, stir in heaping ½ cup (50 g) grated Parmesan along with the seasonings.

This is my ultimate midweek meal as it's packed full of flavor and goodness. Sometimes it's easy to get a little stuck with lunch ideas, and this is also a great dish to make in bulk and take to work in a lunchbox the next day. Kelp noodles are popular in Asian cooking and work brilliantly with fragrant or spicy dishes. They're also a nutritional powerhouse, so dish up and dose up on your vitamins and minerals!

MARINATED TOFU STIR-FRY WITH KELP NOODLES AND ASIAN GREENS

7 oz (200 g) firm tofu, cut into ¾-in (2-cm) cubes
7 oz (200 g) kelp noodles or rice noodles
2 Tbsp coconut oil
8 scallions, cut into matchsticks
1 red bell pepper, seeded and sliced
1 green bell pepper, sliced
1 bok choy or tat soi, chopped
Ground back pepper
Alfalfa sprouts, to serve

FOR THE MARINADE
2 garlic cloves, crushed
1 oz (30 g) piece of ginger, chopped
¼ oz (10 g) fresh horseradish, peeled and chopped
4 tsp sesame oil
6 tsp tamari
3 Tbsp (40 ml) rice wine vinegar

SERVES 2 TO 4

Blitz the marinade ingredients together in a food processor, then transfer to a bowl. Add the cubed tofu to the marinade, stir to coat, then set aside to marinate for at least 2 hours.

Cook the kelp or rice noodles according to the package directions. Once cooked, set the noodles aside. Heat the coconut oil in a wok or heavy-bottom frying pan, then add the tofu along with the marinade and cook for 2 minutes, stirring occasionally. Add the scallions, peppers, and bok choy or tat soi, and cook for 3 minutes.

Meanwhile, submerge the noodles in cold water for 1 minute, then drain and stir into the tofu and vegetables, mixing until the noodles are coated in the sauce. Add black pepper to taste and serve with a sprinkling of alfalfa sprouts.

People are always asking me for lunch ideas, or alternatives to sandwiches and salads, and these fritters are one of my favorites to pack into lunchboxes as a light bite. They work equally well as a side dish or as finger food for relaxed lunches with friends. I serve these fritters with a refreshing tzatziki.

CARROT, SWEET POTATO, AND FETA FRITTERS WITH TZATZIKI

3 large carrots, peeled and grated
1 sweet potato, peeled and grated
1 red onion, peeled and grated
1 garlic clove, crushed
1 heaping tsp ras el hanout (optional)
3 large eggs, beaten
3 Tbsp chickpea flour or other
   gluten-free flour
2/3 cup (100 g) crumbled feta
Handful of fresh parsley
   leaves, chopped
1 Tbsp coconut oil
Himalayan salt and black pepper

FOR THE TZATZIKI
1 garlic clove
1/2 cucumber, peeled and seeded
7 Tbsp (100 g) Greek yogurt
Handful of chopped mint
   (optional)
Himalayan salt and black pepper

SERVES 4

To make the tzatziki, place the garlic with a pinch of salt in a mortar and pestle. Blend to a very fine paste. Grate the peeled cucumber into a clean dish towel, then squeeze to remove as much liquid as possible. Place the cucumber into a bowl, then add the remaining ingredients and combine thoroughly. Place in the refrigerator until ready to serve.

In a large mixing bowl, mix the grated carrots, sweet potato, and red onion, then mix in the garlic and ras el hanout, if using.

In a separate bowl, whisk together the beaten eggs and flour, then stir into the vegetables with the feta and parsley.

Melt the coconut oil in a frying pan over medium heat. Shape the fritter ingredients into patty-size balls, then, working in batches, add to the frying pan and flatten using a spatula.

Cook for about 3 minutes each side, being careful not to burn them. Serve golden and slightly crunchy with a dollop of tzatziki.

FALAFEL BITES

14-oz (400 g) can chickpeas, drained and rinsed
4 tsp coconut oil, plus extra for frying
2 garlic cloves, crushed
1 Tbsp ground cumin
½ tsp ground coriander
Pinch of dried red pepper flakes
Grated zest of ½ lime
½ tsp baking soda
2 scallions, minced
5 tbsp fresh cilantro leaves, chopped
Himalayan salt and black pepper

SERVES 4

When I was little, I used to eat these moreish bites with Indian takeouts or homemade curries, in place of onion bhajis. Now, I like to add them to gluten-free wraps for a nutritious and filling lunch, or I'll just grab them and eat them on-the-go.

Blitz together all the ingredients in a food processor, then tip the mixture into a bowl and place in the refrigerator to firm up, about 30 minutes.

Using dessertspoonsful of mixture, form into flat, round cakes. Place on a baking sheet and refrigerate for 30 minutes.

Heat 2 to 3 Tbsp coconut oil in a large, nonstick frying pan and cook the falafels for about 5 minutes, turning occasionally, until crisp and brown. Lift out with a slotted spoon and drain on paper towels.

Serve with Gluten-Free Flatbreads (see page 183), Sun-Dried Tomato Hummus (see page 178), and Tabbouleh with Tahini Dressing (see below).

TABBOULEH WITH TAHINI DRESSING

Scant ⅔ cup (125 g) buckwheat
¾ cup (180 ml) water
4 tsp coconut oil, melted
5¼ oz (150 g) ripe tomatoes, chopped
2 scallions, finely sliced
Juice of 1 lime
1 tsp Baharat spice mix (see page 181)
3 oz (80 g) fresh Italian parsley sprigs, leaves only
¾ oz (20 g) mint sprigs, leaves only
Himalayan salt and black pepper

FOR THE TAHINI DRESSING
1 garlic clove, crushed
2 Tbsp tahini, stirred well
1 Tbsp coconut oil, melted
Juice of 1 lime
Pinch of Himalayan salt

SERVES 4

Traditionally tabbouleh is made with bulgur, or cracked wheat, but fortunately there are some wonderful wheat- and gluten-free "grains" (which are really seeds), such as quinoa and buckwheat than can be used as substitutes.

Place the buckwheat in a saucepan. Add the ¾ cup (180 ml) water and the coconut oil. Bring to a boil, cover, and then let cook on low heat for 12 to 15 minutes. Alternatively, cook the buckwheat according to the package directions. Once cooked, set the buckwheat aside to cool and transfer to a serving bowl. Add the tomatoes and scallions along with the lime juice and spice mix.

Slice the parsley and mint leaves as finely as possible, using a slicing motion rather than chopping down onto the board, to prevent the flavor seeping out. Add the herbs to the serving bowl and mix. Season to taste.

Blend together all the ingredients for the tahini dressing and serve with the tabbouleh.

This is a wonderful pâté, so simple to make and perfect for serving on gluten-free bread, baked potatoes, or even stirred into soups. A traditional pâté uses butter, which we've substituted with coconut oil so it is great for those who are lactose intolerant. We enjoy this pâté on special occasions, such as an appetizer on Christmas Day, and is my Auntie Judy and Uncle Ron's favorite.

CHICKEN LIVER PÂTÉ

1 cup (200 g) coconut oil,
    plus extra to finish
14 oz (400 g) organic chicken livers,
    cut in half and sinew trimmed off
6 shallots, minced
2 garlic cloves, chopped
2 tsp fresh thyme leaves
1 tsp ground allspice
Himalayan salt and black pepper

TO SERVE
Gluten-free bread, toasted
Gherkins and small pickles
Lemon wedges

SERVES 8

| GF | WF | DF | LF |

Melt scant ¼ cup (50 g) of the coconut oil in a large frying pan. Add the chicken livers and cook over medium heat for 4 to 6 minutes, turning during cooking. Do not overcook, the livers should still be pink on the inside. Remove from the pan using a slotted spoon and set aside.

Melt another scant ¼ cup (50 g) coconut oil in the pan, add the shallots, and fry over medium heat, adding a little more oil if required, until softened; do not let them color.

Stir through the garlic, half the thyme leaves, and the allspice, and cook for 2 minutes. Remove from the heat and add the remaining coconut oil, stirring until melted and combined.

Tip the livers and the shallot mixture into a food processor, with salt and pepper to taste. Process until smooth, then taste and adjust the seasoning if necessary.

Using a spatula, scrape the mixture into a pretty serving bowl, smoothing over the surface. Place in the refrigerator to set for about 1 hour.

Brush the surface of the set pâté with a little more coconut oil and sprinkle over the remaining thyme leaves. Serve with toasted gluten-free bread, gherkins, pickles, and lemon wedges.

This pâté will keep, covered, in the refrigerator for a few days, but I recommend you remove it to room temperature about an hour before eating.

GOAT CHEESE AND ARUGULA FRITTATA

1 Tbsp coconut oil
2 red onions, thinly sliced
2 large garlic cloves, crushed
7 oz (200 g) arugula
2 Tbsp chopped fresh parsley
2 Tbsp Sun-Dried Tomato Pesto
   (see page 178)
6 large eggs, lightly beaten
1/3 cup (75 g) soft goat cheese
3 Tbsp freshly grated Parmesan
Himalayan salt and black pepper

SERVES 4

There's something about the classic combination of goat cheese and arugula that I never grow bored of—it just works. This frittata is great for a cheap and fast evening meal but makes a healthy and filling lunch, too. For an added kick, serve with my Raspberry Chipotle Sauce (see page 176).

Preheat the broiler on medium setting. Melt half of the coconut oil in a heavy-bottom pan, add the onions, and sauté over medium heat until soft. Add the garlic and cook for another 2 minutes, then tip into a mixing bowl, add the arugula, parsley, and pesto, mix together, then add the eggs.

   Melt the remaining coconut oil in the frying pan until hot, then pour the mixture into the pan and cook for 2 to 3 minutes, or until the mixture just starts to set. Sprinkle the goat cheese and Parmesan over the top and cook for another 2 minutes.

   Place the pan under the broiler for 3 to 5 minutes, or until the top is golden and bubbling. Let stand for 5 minutes before cutting into wedges and serving.

SWEET POTATO AND CHILE FRITTATA WITH FETA

1 sweet potato, peeled and diced
1 Tbsp coconut oil
1 green chile, seeded and sliced
6 large eggs, beaten
Small handful of fresh cilantro
   leaves, chopped
1¾ oz (50 g) feta
Himalayan salt and black pepper
Arugula, to serve

SERVES 4

When I was working as a beauty therapist full time, I would often make a frittata the night before, ready to enjoy the next day while at work. It lasts well and tastes just as good cold as hot, making it perfect for your lunchbox.

Steam the sweet potato over a pan of boiling water for 10 to 15 minutes, or until softened.

   Preheat the broiler on medium setting. Melt the coconut oil in an ovenproof frying pan over medium heat, addthe sweet potato and chile, and sauté for 3 to 4 minutes.

   Mix the eggs and cilantro together in a pitcher, then pour over the sweet potato and chile, before crumbling over the feta. Cook for 2 to 3 minutes, or until the base is just starting to set, then place the pan under the broiler until the top is cooked. Let stand for 5 minutes before cutting into wedges and serving with a handful of arugula.

I love omelets and I couldn't choose just one to share with you, so instead I decided to give you three. Have a go at mixing and matching ingredients to make this basic recipe all the more interesting. Serve with a green salad.

WE'RE TALKING OMELETS! THREE RECIPES IN ONE

GF WF

1 tsp coconut oil
3 large eggs, beaten
Himalayan salt and black pepper

SALMON AND SAMPHIRE
⅓ cup (20 g) crumbled feta
Pinch of dried red pepper flakes
Handful of samphire
Smoked salmon

ROASTED VEGETABLE AND GOAT CHEESE
1 Tbsp roasted vegetables
1 Tbsp cooked sweet potatoes
1 jalapeño chile, seeded and sliced
¾ oz (20 g) goat cheese
Small handful of parsley, chopped

MY ITALIAN OMELET
1 small onion, sliced
1 tomato, sliced
Basil leaves
Mozzarella, torn into pieces
1 tsp dried oregano

SERVES 1

SALMON AND SAMPHIRE
Melt the coconut oil in a frying pan, then add the eggs and season to taste. Sprinkle over the feta and red pepper flakes and gently cook for a couple of minutes. Flip the omelet over and cook the other side. Add the samphire and smoked salmon. Fold the omelet in half before serving immediately.

ROASTED VEGETABLE AND GOAT CHEESE
Melt the coconut oil in a frying pan and add the roasted vegetables and cooked sweet potato. Sauté until lightly browned, then add the eggs along with the remaining ingredients, before seasoning and cooking on each side.

MY ITALIAN OMELET
Melt the coconut oil in a frying pan and sauté the onion and tomato until softened. Add the eggs, basil, mozzarella, and oregano, before seasoning and cooking on each side.

QUICK
SUPPERS

This dish is quick to whip up after a long day at work, and tastes amazing—I love the combination of flavors, from the salty olives to the sweetness of the sun-dried tomatoes. Feel free to use different nuts, such as hazelnuts, in the stuffing, which works equally well with fish as with chicken. If you have any of the stuffing mixture left over, it will keep for up to one week when kept in the refrigerator.

CHICKEN BREAST WITH OLIVE, SAGE, AND WALNUTS

4 boneless and skinless
   chicken breasts
½ cup (100 g) black pitted olives
1 garlic clove, crushed
Handful of fresh sage leaves
¾ cup (75 g) walnuts or pecans
1 Tbsp coconut oil, plus a
   little extra, melted, to drizzle
2½ oz (70 g) sun-dried tomatoes

FOR THE TOPPING
2 slices of gluten-free bread
Handful of fresh parsley leaves
¾ oz (20 g) Parmesan

SERVES 4

GF   WF

Preheat the oven to 350°F (180°C). Line a baking sheet with parchment paper.

Cut a slit along the side of each chicken breast to form a pocket. Blitz the remaining ingredients together in a food processor, then stuff into the chicken pockets and transfer to the lined sheet.

To make the topping, blitz the ingredients together in a food processor. Sprinkle over the chicken breasts, drizzle with a little melted coconut oil, then cook in the oven for 20 to 25 minutes, until cooked through (see below).

Serve with Roasted Sweet Potato Wedges (see page 120) and seasonal vegetables.

TIP One of my most used kitchen gadgets is a good meat thermometer, which means you can wave goodbye to dry, overcooked chicken. It also works a treat if you worry about undercooking, too. Chicken is cooked when the center of the thickest piece reaches 165°F (74°C). It is best to cook meat from room temperature rather than straight from the refrigerator, but don't let it sit out for too long—15 to 20 minutes will do.

CHICKEN MASALA SKEWERS

4 boneless, skinless chicken breasts,
   cubed or cut into bite-size pieces

FOR THE MARINADE
½ tsp cumin seeds
½ tsp coriander seeds
½ tsp grated lime zest
½ tsp dried mint
1 Tbsp coconut oil, melted
Juice of 1 lime
7 Tbsp (100 ml) Greek yogurt
Thumb-size piece of ginger,
   peeled and finely grated
1 garlic clove, peeled and crushed
1 green chile, seeded and sliced
1 green bell pepper, finely chopped
Himalayan salt and black pepper

TO SERVE
Handful of fresh cilantro leaves,
   chopped
Handful of fresh mint leaves, chopped
Lime wedges

SERVES 4

For all you fans of Indian food and takeouts, these fantastic skewers are a healthy option and are great on the barbecue, or as a finger food served with my Carrot, Sweet Potato, and Feta Fritters (see page 57), or with my Fruity Mango Salsa (see page 182) and a salad with Lemon Garlic Dressing (see page 175).

Preheat the oven to 250°F (120°C).
   Spread the cumin and coriander seeds and the lime zest out on a baking sheet and toast in the oven for about 10 minutes. Grind to a coarse powder using a mortar and pestle. Add the ground spices to the remaining marinade ingredients in a large mixing bowl, then season well and stir. Add the chicken pieces. Cover and refrigerate overnight, for the chicken to marinate.
   When ready to cook, preheat the overhead broiler to hot or light the barbecue and wait until it is at high heat. Thread the chicken pieces onto four metal skewers. Grill or barbecue for 8 to 10 minutes, turning regularly. The chicken may seem to brown quite quickly, but don't be tempted to turn the skewers too soon, as you want it to caramelize them and release all those wonderful flavors.
   Serve the chicken skewers immediately with the fresh herbs and lime wedges.

CHICKEN SATAY

4 boneless, skinless chicken breasts,
   cubed or cut into bite-size pieces

FOR THE SATAY
⅞ cup (200 ml) coconut milk
6 Tbsp natural peanut butter
Thumb-size piece of ginger,
   peeled and grated (optional, but
   adds a little spice)
1 Tbsp tahini
1 Tbsp gluten-free soy sauce
1 tsp dried red pepper flakes
2 tsp coconut oil, plus extra for frying
Juice of 1 lime
1 garlic clove, peeled

SERVES 4 TO 6

With its amazing flavors, this is an absolute favorite with Willis and I. The takeout versions tend to be loaded with hidden nasties and sugars, so I made it my mission to turn this delicious dish into a nutritious meal.

Put the satay ingredients into a blender and process until smooth, then transfer to a bowl.
   Melt a little coconut oil in a frying pan over high heat. Dunk each chicken cube into the sauce, before adding to the frying pan. Fry for 8 to 10 minutes, turning frequently, until cooked through. Once cooked, serve with brown rice and fresh vegetables.

VARIATIONS
Instead of dunking the chicken cubes in the satay before frying, you can serve the satay alongside as a dipping sauce. For a barbecue, thread the chicken cubes onto skewers and cook for 8 to 10 minutes over high heat.

Ginger, lemongrass, and chile go so well together, and the smell you get when cooking these in Lucy Bee coconut oil is truly mouthwatering.

CHICKEN WITH LEMONGRASS, LIME, AND CILANTRO

1 Tbsp coconut oil
Thumb-size piece of ginger,
    peeled and grated
2 lemongrass stalks, thinly sliced
1 red chile, seeded and chopped
6 kaffir lime leaves
1²/₃ cups (400 ml) coconut milk
2 tsp sugar (palm, coconut, or any
    natural alternative)
4 boneless, skinless chicken thighs
1 Tbsp lime juice
Handful of fresh cilantro leaves,
    coarsely chopped, to serve

SERVES 4

Melt the coconut oil in a frying pan, then add the ginger, lemongrass, and chile and gently sauté.

Stir in the lime leaves, coconut milk, and sugar, then bring to a gentle simmer and cook, uncovered, at a relaxed bubble for around 5 minutes.

Add the chicken, then cover and simmer for about 25 minutes, until tender and cooked. Stir in the lime juice and sprinkle the cilantro over before serving with brown rice and steamed broccoli.

This dish combines two of my favorite ingredients—chicken and chorizo—and is the perfect meal to eat al fresco, while pretending you're on vacation in the Mediterranean. It also tastes just as good the next day eaten cold, as the flavors are enhanced.

CHICKEN AND CHORIZO PAELLA

Scant ¼ cup (40 g) coconut oil
1 onion, minced
7 oz (200 g) cooking chorizo, chopped
4 garlic cloves, crushed
2 cups (400 g) risotto or paella rice
1 level tsp smoked paprika (sweet or hot)
7 oz (200 g) roasted red bell peppers from a jar, diced
10½ oz (300 g) boneless, skinless chicken breasts, cut into bite-size pieces
2 cups (500 ml) chicken broth
2 cups (500 ml) water
Large pinch of saffron threads
5¼ oz (150 g) cooked fava beans, skinned (frozen are fine)
12 black olives (optional)
Handful of fresh parsley leaves
Himalayan salt and black pepper
Lemons wedges, to serve

SERVES 4

Melt the coconut oil in a large, heavy-bottom pan and gently fry the onion and chorizo, until the onion has softened. Add the garlic and sauté for another minute.

Tip in the rice, stir, and cook for 1 minute. Add the smoked paprika, red pepper, and chicken and stir it all together.

Pour in the broth, water, saffron, fava beans, and olives, if using, then season to taste. Reduce the heat to low, cover, and cook for 12 to 15 minutes, stirring occasionally—but as little as possible—to prevent sticking. Add the parsley, let stand for a few minutes, and serve with lemon wedges, and a green salad.

PAN-FRIED MARINATED SALMON WITH WILTED BABY SPINACH

FOR THE MARINADE
Thumb-size piece of ginger, peeled
1 garlic clove, peeled
4 tsp (20 ml) tamari sauce
Juice of 1 lime

2 salmon fillets
4 tsp coconut oil
3 oz (80 g) baby spinach leaves

SERVES 2

Salmon is not only incredibly good for your body, skin, and hair, but it's also really quick to prepare. This simple marinade really lifts the salmon fillets too, taking them from delicious to out of this world.

Blitz together the ginger, garlic, tamari, and lime juice in a food processor. Place the salmon fillets in a bowl, cover with the mixture, and let marinate for 30 minutes.

Melt the coconut oil in a heavy-bottom frying pan, then add the salmon skin-side down, along with the marinade, and fry for 8 minutes, turning halfway through.

Remove to serving plates and keep warm. Add the spinach to the pan and cook until wilted, 3 to 4 minutes. Add the spinach to the plates alongside the salmon and serve with either rice or quinoa and cherry tomatoes.

VARIATION
For an alternative marinade, use 1 tsp sumac, 1 tsp toasted fennel seeds, and the zest and juice of 1 lime.

SALMON WITH PESTO TOPPING

Coconut oil, for greasing
3½ oz (100 g) Sun-Dried Tomato
   Pesto (page 178), or store-bought
½ cup (50 g) gluten-free bread crumbs
2 salmon fillets

SERVES 2

GF | WF | DF | LF

This looks like a really impressive dish, but it's surprisingly quick to make. It's packed full of the most wonderful flavors and makes the perfect light lunch or supper to enjoy alfresco in the summer.

Preheat the oven to 350°F (180°C). Lightly grease a baking sheet using a little coconut oil. Mix together the pesto and bread crumbs.

Place the salmon fillets skin-side down on the baking sheet and spread the pesto mixture evenly on top. Cook in the oven for 20 minutes, or until the salmon is just cooked through.

Serve at once with Sweet Potato Mash with Chives (see page 119) and broccoli or asparagus, or with new potatoes lightly crushed with nori flakes and drizzled with coconut oil, and sautéed samphire.

FISH FINGERS

3 slices of gluten-free bread
1 garlic clove, peeled
1¾ oz (50 g) Parmesan
¾ oz (20 g) fresh parsley
½ cup (60 g) gluten-free flour,
   seasoned
1 egg, beaten
12¼ oz (350 g) cod loin, cut into
   finger-size pieces
¼ cup (50 g) coconut oil
Himalayan salt and black pepper
Lemon wedges, to serve

SERVES 2

These delicious, golden fish fingers are another wonderful unhealthy-to-healthy recipe—your friends won't complain if you dish these up for supper!

Put the bread, garlic, Parmesan, and parsley in a food processor and blitz until it resembles fine bread crumbs. Tip into a dish, and then place the seasoned flour in a separate dish. Pour the beaten egg into a third dish.

Take one piece of fish and dip it into the flour, giving it a light shake to remove excess flour and making sure it is evenly coated, then into the egg. Toss it in the bread crumb mixture and set aside on a cutting board. Repeat with the remaining pieces of fish.

Heat the coconut oil in a heavy-bottom frying pan. When hot (test by dropping a few crumbs into the oil; they should sizzle) add the fish fingers. Fry for 2 to 3 minutes, then turn and cook for a few minutes, until golden. Transfer to a plate lined with paper towels to blot off any excess oil. Season and serve with Roasted Sweet Potato Wedges (see page 120), Tzatziki (see page 57), and a green salad.

TURKEY BURGERS

1¾ oz (50 g) red onions, minced
Juice of 2 limes
8¾ oz (250 g) ground turkey
1 large egg
⅓ cup (50 g) crumbled feta
Pinch of paprika
Pinch of dried red pepper flakes
1 tsp coconut oil
Himalayan salt and black pepper

**SERVES 2 (MAKES 4 MEDIUM
BURGERS)**

Everyone loves a good burger, don't they? With added bacon, cheese, and other toppings, they're not always the healthiest option. These turkey burgers are lovely and light and are a great midweek supper alternative.

Put the onions into a small bowl, add half the lime juice, cover, and let soak overnight in the refrigerator. (This will give the burgers a delicious, zesty, sweet flavor.)

Put the ground turkey in a bowl with the egg, feta, paprika, pepper flakes, and soaked onions. Season well, then mix together using a wooden spoon, or your hands. Divide the mixture into three and shape into burgers, making sure each burger is compact and holds together.

Melt the coconut oil in a frying pan over medium heat and, when hot, add the burgers and cook for 5 minutes, adding a dash of the remaining lime juice to the pan. Turn and fry for another few minutes until cooked through. If necessary, turn them again, so that they are cooked evenly on both sides.

Remove from the heat and squeeze over more lime juice. Season and serve with Roasted Sweet Potato Wedges (see page 120), Tzatziki (see page 57), and a green salad.

ZUCCHINI AND SHRIMP

10½ oz (300 g) zucchini, trimmed
7 oz (200 g) carrots, peeled
1 Tbsp coconut oil
1 oz (30 g) ginger, peeled and grated
½ red chile, seeded and minced
2 garlic cloves, crushed
24 raw shrimp, peeled and
    deveined (tails on)
10 scallions, minced

FOR THE DRESSING
Heaping 2½ Tbsp (40 ml) sesame oil
¼ cup (30 g) cashews
2 Tbsp cashew nut butter
4 tsp (20 ml) tamari sauce
Juice of 2 limes
Heaping 2½ Tbsp (40 ml) rice
    wine vinegar
2 tsp agave nectar

SERVES 2

Pasta made from zucchini, is one of those miraculous, healthy foods that I enjoy with pretty much everything. It amazes me that you can make something so delicious from a simple zucchini.

Blitz the dressing ingredients together in a blender, adding a drop of water to loosen it if necessary.

Using a spiralizer, make "spaghetti" from the zucchini and carrots. If you don't have one, cut the zucchini and carrots lengthwise as thinly as possible, then across into very fine strands.

Heat the coconut oil in a wok or heavy-bottom frying pan, add the ginger, chille, and garlic and cook for 1 minute, stirring occasionally. Add the shrimp and cook for 5 minutes, or just until they turn pink (don't overcook them), stirring every now and again. Remove from the pan.

Add the zucchini and carrots to the pan, then add the dressing, mix everything together well to coat in the dressing. Cook gently for another 1 minute. Serve immediately, with the scallions and shrimp piled on top.

COCONUT SHRIMP

20 raw shrimp, peeled and deveined
    (tails on, heads removed)
⅓ cup (40 g) cornstarch
1 large egg, beaten
Scant ¼ cup (20 g) gluten-free bread
    crumbs mixed with scant ½ cup
    (40 g) dried shredded coconut and
    a pinch each of Himalayan salt and
    black pepper
Scant ¼ cup (40 g) coconut oil

TO SERVE
1 bunch of fresh cilantro, leaves
    chopped
Chili Dipping Sauce (see page 175)

SERVES 2

The flavors in this wonderfully light dish really remind me of exotic vacations and gorgeous sunshine; tropical island eating at its best. You can just keep this very simple, and serve with lemon wedges.

Devein the shrimp by making a shallow cut along the length of each and removing any black line, using the tip of a knife.

Put the cornstarch, egg, and bread crumb mixture into three separate dishes. One shrimp at a time, dip into the cornstarch, then into the egg, then into the bread crumb mixture. Place on a plate until all the shrimp are coated.

Heat the coconut oil in a frying pan until really hot (check by dropping few crumbs into the oil; they should sizzle), then add the shrimp to the pan and cook over high heat for 3 to 4 minutes. Turn and cook for the same time on the other side.

Serve immediately, sprinkled with chopped cilantro, and with the Chili Dipping Sauce.

SAUTÉED SQUID WITH POTATOES AND CHILI

¼ cup (60 g) coconut oil, plus a
   little extra for the squid
5¼ oz (150 g) red onion, finely sliced
12¼ oz (350 g) cooked waxy
potatoes, cut into bite-size pieces
2 to 3 garlic cloves, minced
1 lb 2 oz (500 g) squid, sliced
   into rings
½ tsp dried red pepper flakes
1 Tbsp sherry vinegar
Big handful of coarsely chopped
   fresh parsley and cilantro
Lime wedges, to serve

**SERVES 8 TO 10 AS AN APPETIZER
OR 4 TO 6 AS A MAIN COURSE**

GF   WF   DF   LF

**Go back five or so years and you would have
struggled to buy squid easily. Happily, most grocery
stores now sell squid—and if you have a local fish
supplier, even better! Squid always reminds me of
being on vacation, so whenever I have it at home,
those vacation memories come flooding right back.**

Melt the coconut oil in a large, heavy-bottom frying
pan. Add the onion and gently sauté until soft, then
add the potatoes and continue to cook until the onions
and potatoes are just browning (not burned!), stirring
occasionally.
   Add the garlic and cook for 2 to 3 minutes, stirring
often to mix, then remove from the pan and set aside.
Add a little more coconut oil to the pan, stir in the squid
and red pepper flakes and cook for 3 to 5 minutes, taking
care not to overcook the squid or it will be tough.
   Return the potatoes and garlic to the pan, then add the
sherry vinegar and herbs. Give everything a good stir to
combine and serve with lime wedges to squeeze over,
and a crisp Boston lettuce salad.

SALT AND PEPPER SQUID

12¼ oz (350 g) cleaned squid tubes
⅓ cup (40 g) cornstarch
⅓ cup (40 g) gluten-free flour
Scant ¼ cup (50 g) coconut oil
Himalayan salt and black pepper
Lemon wedges or Chili Dipping
   Sauce (see page 175), to serve

SERVES 2 TO 4

GF   WF   DF   LF

**I never normally feel left out simply because I can't
eat gluten, but when I see squid on the menu in
restaurants, this soon changes, as I long to eat it.
This gluten-free version has made my life complete!**

Cut the squid into thin strips. Mix the flours together in
a bowl with 1 tsp salt and 2 tsp pepper, then dip the
squid into the flour and give it a light shake to remove
any excess.
   Heat the coconut oil in a heavy-bottom frying pan.
When hot (test by dropping a small piece of bread into
the oil; it should sizzle), add the squid to the pan, and fry
for 2 to 3 minutes, then turn and cook for another couple
of minutes on the other side.
   Transfer to a plate lined with paper towels, season with
salt and pepper, and serve immediately, with lemon juice
squeezed over or with the Chili Dipping Sauce.

BROWN RICE SPAGHETTI
WITH WILD GARLIC

1 lb 2 oz (500 g) Rizopia organic
  brown rice spaghetti
½ cup (100 g) coconut oil
2 plump garlic cloves, minced
1¾ oz (50 g) wild garlic leaves
  (when in season)
Handful of chopped fresh parsley
Himalayan sea salt and black pepper

SERVES 4

GF | WF | DF | LF | V

This recipe is so easy to make after a tough day at
work. Sometimes we can get a little carried away
with complex flavors or fancy ingredients, but often
I find that simpler dishes taste much nicer. This is one
of those amazing, memorable meals that combines
simple, stunning flavors with comforting spaghetti.

Heat the coconut oil in a frying pan, add the garlic cloves,
and gently fry until golden but not burned, then add salt
and pepper to taste.

   Meanwhile, cook the spaghetti according to the
package directions. Transfer to a warmed serving bowl.
Tip the garlicky oil onto the spaghetti, then add the wild
garlic leaves (if using), chopped parsley, mix well, and
serve immediately.

BROWN RICE SPAGHETTI WITH
ANCHOVY AND TOMATO SAUCE

½ cup (100 g) coconut oil, plus a
  little extra for the greens
1 plump garlic clove, minced
1¾-oz (50-g) can anchovies in oil
Handful of chopped parsley, plus
  extra to serve
14-oz (400-g) can chopped
  tomatoes
1 lb 2 oz (500 g) Rizopia organic
  brown rice spaghetti
Himalayan salt and black pepper

SERVES 4

GF | WF | DF | LF

This is another fast and easy recipe. You can go from
oven to plate in just 20 minutes, and it's so intensely
satisfying and full of flavor. It tastes great on its own
but, for an added health kick, serve with broccoli or
a green salad, and a fine grating of Parmesan.

Melt the coconut oil in a large frying pan, add the garlic,
and fry gently until golden brown but not burned. Add
the anchovy fillets and their oil, which will dissolve nicely,
then the parsley, and stir for 1 minute before tipping in
the tomatoes with pepper to taste. Simmer, uncovered,
for 20 minutes.

   Meanwhile, cook the spaghetti according to the
package directions. Transfer to a warmed serving bowl.
Pour the anchovy and tomato sauce over the spaghetti,
sprinkle with extra parsley, and serve immediately.

A satisfying quick supper that is the perfect pick-me-up after a long day. Sometimes I even make extra so that I can eat any leftovers for breakfast the next day.

EGG-FRIED WILD RICE WITH EDAMAME

Scant ½ cup (80 g) wild rice
3½ oz (100 g) fresh edamame
    beans, shelled
1 Tbsp coconut oil
3 oz (80 g) chard, shredded
2 Tbsp pumpkin seeds
1 egg, beaten

SERVES 2

Rinse the rice, then cook according to the package directions. Blanch the edamame beans in boiling water until tender, then drain.

Heat the coconut oil in a wok and add the chard and pumpkin seeds. Once the chard is wilted, add the drained rice and edamame beans, mixing everything together.

Stir the beaten egg through the rice for 1 to 2 minutes before serving immediately.

This nutritious brown rice bowl topped with fresh, seared tuna is clean eating at its very best—wholesome and tasty.

SEARED TUNA AND SESAME RICE BOWL

1 cup (200 g) short-grain brown rice
Pinch of Himalayan salt
4 tsp nori flakes
2 tsp coconut oil
2 small, thick tuna steaks
1 avocado, peeled and sliced
½ cucumber, peeled, seeded, and sliced into thin batons
2 Tbsp black sesame seeds, toasted in a dry pan
Handful of fresh cilantro, leaves only, chopped
Pickled ginger, to serve

FOR THE DRESSING
Juice of ½ lemon
Juice of ½ orange
1 tsp manuka honey
2 Tbsp tamari sauce
½ Tbsp gluten-free fish sauce
1 Tbsp brown rice vinegar

SERVES 4

Cook the rice in about double its volume of water with the salt for 40 minutes, or until tender. Drain, transfer to a large mixing bowl, and stir through the nori flakes.

Meanwhile, in a small bowl, mix the lemon and orange juice, honey, tamari, fish sauce, and brown rice vinegar together to make a dressing.

Heat the coconut oil in a griddle pan to fairly high heat, add the tuna steaks, and sear for about 30 to 45 seconds on each side (the middle should still be pink). Remove to a board to rest for a couple of minutes, before slicing into thin pieces.

Divide the rice, avocado, cucumber, and tuna slices between deep bowls. Sprinkle over the black sesame seeds, pour over the dressing, top with fresh cilantro, and serve, with pickled ginger.

SLOW COOK
WEEKENDS

This is the perfect alternative to Sunday roasts and is a real treat for family dinners come the end of the week. I just love the French-style creamy sauce, which tastes delicious with mashed potato. Perfect for indulging!

TARRAGON ROAST CHICKEN

1 chicken, about 3¼ lb (1.5 kg)
Scant ¼ cup (50 g) coconut oil
½ lemon
1 large bunch of fresh tarragon
Himalayan salt and black pepper
Chopped chives, to serve

FOR THE SAUCE

6 shallots, minced
1 garlic clove, crushed
⅝ cup (150 ml) white wine vinegar
⅞ cup (200 ml) chicken broth
   (see page 181)
3 tsp Dijon mustard
¼ cup (60 ml) light cream
⅓ cup (20 g) chopped fresh
   tarragon leaves

SERVES 4

Preheat the oven to 400°F (200°C).

Prepare the chicken for roasting by rubbing it all over with the coconut oil. Put the chicken in a roasting tray and place the lemon half and tarragon inside the chicken. Season well, transfer to the oven, and roast for 1¼ to 1½ hours, or until the juices run clear when the thickest part of the leg is pierced with a skewer. Remove the chicken from the roasting tray and keep warm.

Place the tray over medium heat and add the shallots, garlic, and vinegar. Cook until softened, scraping any tasty bits from the bottom of the pan.

Add the chicken broth and mustard, stir together, and reduce for about 5 minutes. Gradually add the cream and warm through before sprinkling in the chopped tarragon.

Carve the chicken. Serve with the tarragon sauce, sprinkled with chopped chives, and accompanied by either Roast Potatoes (see page 118) or Potato and Celeriac Mash (see page 119) and steamed broccoli.

I have always used whole spices instead of ready-made mixes, as I find that this adds a real depth of flavor and I know the spices are fresh. They also work out so much cheaper. Just remember to use your recycled Lucy Bee jar to store your spices in.

HEALTHY CHICKEN CURRY WITH TOMATOES AND GREEN CHILE

2 garlic cloves, peeled
Thumb-size piece of ginger, peeled
1 Tbsp coconut oil, softened
1 large onion, chopped
2 tsp cumin seeds
1 tsp ground turmeric
1 bay leaf
1 blade of mace
2 tsp ground coriander
14-oz (400-g) can chopped
   tomatoes
2 green chiles, halved and seeded
15¾ oz (450 g) skinless chicken
   thighs
2 tsp dried fenugreek leaves
1 tsp garam masala (see page 181)
1 Tbsp Greek yogurt
Handful of chopped fresh cilantro
Himalayan sea salt and black pepper

SERVES 4

Put the garlic and ginger into a small food processor with a little water and blitz to a smooth paste.

Put the coconut oil and onion in a heavy-bottom, large frying pan and cook over medium heat until golden brown.

Add the cumin seeds and stir for a minute, then stir in the turmeric, bay leaf, mace, and ground coriander and cook for 1 minute. Add the garlic-ginger paste, stir, and cook for a couple of minutes—enjoy the wonderful aroma!

Tip in the tomatoes and simmer for a few moments until well mixed (you may need to add a little water), then add the chiles (you can pick them out at the end if you are concerned about the heat) with salt and pepper to taste. Add the chicken, cover, and cook over low heat at a gentle bubble for 1½ hours.

Stir in the dried fenugreek and garam masala, then spoon into bowls. Top with the yogurt, sprinkle over the cilantro, and serve with brown rice.

This is my dad's favorite dish, and pretty much everyone else loves it, too. The spices used here are great for healing and cleansing the body, while the rich flavors make it deliciously warming—perfect for cozying up with on a cold winter night.

TARKA DHAL WITH TURMERIC AND CORIANDER

FOR THE DHAL
1 cup (200 g) red split lentils
4½ cups (1 liter) water
4 slices of ginger, peel on
1 tsp ground turmeric
1 tsp Himalayan salt
14-oz (400-g) can tomatoes
4 Tbsp fresh cilantro leaves

FOR THE TARKA
3 Tbsp coconut oil
4 garlic cloves, sliced
½ tsp asafetida
2 tsp cumin seeds
2 tsp ground coriander
3 green chiles, left whole or
    seeded and sliced

SERVES 4

| GF | WF | DF | LF | V |

Rinse the lentils well under cold running water, then tip into a pan with the water. Bring to a boil, then skim off the scum and add the ginger slices and turmeric. Cover, leaving the lid slightly ajar, and simmer over low heat for 1½ hours, until soft and a thick oatmeal consistency, stirring often to ensure it doesn't catch.

Remove the ginger slices, then add the salt and chopped tomatoes. Set aside and keep warm.

To make the tarka, melt the coconut oil in a small frying pan. Add the garlic and fry until golden. Stir in the asafetida, cumin seeds, ground coriander, and chiles, then pour into the lentil mixture. Finally, add the cilantro and serve with boiled rice.

At home, we call this recipe Chicken Mess, but in fact it is a fattee, which is an Arabic word for crumbled. The layers in this dish tend to be crispy flatbreads, and we make our own gluten-free versions, but store-bought gluten-free pitas or wraps are fine here.

CHICKEN FATTEE   GF | WF

4 gluten-free flatbreads (see page 183)
Coconut oil, for brushing and frying
Scant 1 cup (190 g) brown rice
2 boneless, skinless chicken breasts

FOR THE EGGPLANT SAUCE

2 medium eggplants, cut into
    ¾-in (2-cm) cubes
About 4 Tbsp coconut oil
2 garlic cloves, minced
14-oz (400-g) can chopped
    tomatoes
1 tsp coconut sugar
1 tsp ground cinnamon
1 Tbsp tomato paste
14-oz (400-g) can chickpeas,
    well rinsed
Himalayan salt and black pepper

FOR THE YOGURT TOPPING

1 small garlic clove, peeled
Pinch of Himalayan salt
1 cup (250 g) Greek yogurt

TO SERVE

Handful of fresh parsley leaves,
    chopped
1 Tbsp pine nuts, toasted in a dry pan

SERVES 4

Preheat the overhead broiler to hot, brush the flatbreads with coconut oil, and broil for about 5 minutes until crisp.

For the yogurt topping, mash the garlic to a paste with the salt, using a mortar and pestle or by squashing it on a board using the flat side of a large knife. Put the yogurt in a bowl, add the garlic, and mix until smooth.

For the sauce, melt 2 Tbsp coconut oil in a large frying pan and fry the eggplant until soft, adding more oil if needed. Set aside.

Melt another 2 Tbsp coconut oil in the same pan and gently fry the garlic until soft and starting to turn golden. Add the chopped tomatoes, sugar, cinnamon, and tomato paste and cook gently for 15 to 20 minutes, adding a little water if it becomes too thick. Return the eggplant to the pan with the chickpeas and stir to mix. Adjust the seasoning and set aside. Meanwhile, cook the rice according to the package directions.

Slice the chicken breasts in half horizontally, by placing the palm of your hand on the breast and using a sharp knife to slice across, taking great care as you cut. Slice each halved fillet lengthwise into thin strips.

Melt 1 Tbsp coconut oil in the frying pan. Season the chicken, add to the hot oil, and quickly fry until cooked, about 5 minutes each side. Remove and set aside.

Using one big serving dish, start with a layer of broken-up crisp flatbreads then add a layer of the eggplant sauce. Add the rice, then the sauce, followed by the chicken strips. Finally, add the yogurt topping and sprinkle over the parsley and pine nuts.

BARBECUE SPICED LAMB

15¾ oz (450 g) lamb neck slices,
  cubed or cut into bite-size pieces
Juice of 1–2 limes
1 Tbsp ground coriander seeds
1 Tbsp ground cumin
1 tsp ground cinnamon
½ cup (125 ml) Greek yogurt
4 tsp coconut oil

SERVES 2

Don't be put off by the fact that this takes hours
to prepare—I promise that it's well worth waiting
for! The marinating time allows the spices to really
permeate the lamb, leaving the most mouthwatering
flavors imaginable.

In a glass or nonreactive bowl, combine the lamb and lime
juice, then cover, refrigerate, and marinate for 2 hours.
  Drain the juices from the meat and pat it dry. Mix the
spices with the yogurt in a large bowl, and then add the
lamb, before covering and marinating in the refrigerator
for another 4 hours.
  Remove the lamb from the yogurt and, if cooking
on a barbecue, thread onto skewers. Brush with a
little coconut oil, then cook on the barbecue, turning
frequently to avoid burning. Alternatively, heat the
coconut oil in a large frying pan and fry the lamb,
in batches if necessary to avoid overcrowding, over
medium to high heat, until cooked to your liking,
10 to 20 minutes.
  Serve either just as it is, or with Roasted Sweet Potato
Wedges (see page 120), Tzatziki (see page 57), and a
green salad.

COCONUT RICE WITH CARDAMOM SEEDS

2 Tbsp coconut oil
1 cup (200 g) short-grain brown rice
⅞ cup (200 ml) coconut milk
⅞ cup (200 ml) water
Seeds from 10 cardamom pods
Pinch of dried red pepper flakes
  (optional)

SERVES 2 TO 4

The cardamom and coconut flavors complement each
other in this rich, satisfying dish. While I love it as an
indulgent side (try it with Pan-Fried Marinated Salmon
on page 76, or Chicken with Lemongrass, Lime,
and Cilantro on page 72), it works equally well as a
breakfast—think of it as a savory spiced oatmeal!

Melt the coconut oil in a heavy-bottom pan, then add the
rice and stir to coat it in the oil. Tip in the coconut milk,
water, cardamom seeds, and red pepper flakes, if using,
and cook according to the package directions, checking
occasionally as it may need a splash more water.

This dish is a great comfort food for a cold night in, especially after a long afternoon walk. Pop it in the oven before you go, ready for you to return home to a welcoming and enticing aroma! If you manage not to eat it all, then it freezes really well, which in fact helps to intensify the flavor.

LAMB AND SPINACH KORAI

Scant ¾ cup (150 g) coconut oil
1 lb 4 oz (550 g) onions, chopped
14-oz (400-g) can tomatoes
½ cup (120 ml) water
1¾ oz (50 g) ginger, peeled and chopped
2¼ oz (65 g) garlic cloves, chopped
2 lb (900 g) boneless shoulder or leg of lamb, cut into 1½-in (4-cm) cubes
1 tsp Himalayan salt
1 Tbsp ground turmeric
1 Tbsp chili powder
1 Tbsp ground cumin
1 Tbsp paprika
1 Tbsp ground coriander
12¼ oz (350 g) spinach leaves
4 medium green chiles, stalks removed, left whole
1 cup (50 g) chopped fresh cilantro
½ Tbsp garam masala (see page 181)

SERVES 4

Heat the coconut oil in a large, heavy-bottom pan. Add the onions and cook over medium heat for 20 minutes, stirring now and then, until soft and light brown.

Put the tomatoes, water, ginger, and garlic into a food processor and blend until smooth. Using a slotted spoon, transfer the cooked onions to the paste and blend briefly until smooth.

Return the paste to the coconut oil left in the pan, then stir in the lamb and salt. Simmer for 30 minutes, then stir in the turmeric, chili powder, cumin, paprika, and ground coriander and cook until the lamb is tender, 30 to 45 minutes if using shoulder or 45 to 60 if using leg. Add a little water now and then if the sauce starts to stick.

Put half the spinach leaves into a large pan and cook until wilted. Blitz with a little water in the food processor, to a smooth puree. Add to the sauce with the remaining spinach leaves and cook for 2 minutes.

Rinse out the food processor, tip in the whole chiles and 2 to 3 Tbsp water, and blend until smooth. Taste the curry and add as much of this chili puree as you wish, depending on how hot you like it. Alternatively, put a bowl of chili puree on the table and allow each person to add as much as they like.

Stir in the cilantro and garam masala, then transfer to a serving dish just before serving, with Tarka Dhal (see page 95) or Indian-Style Potatoes (see page 118).

This light but satisfying fish curry is the perfect sharing dish for an evening in with friends. Any fish with firm, white flesh works well in this dish, but for a special indulgence use monkfish fillets and even add a few extra shrimp.

KERALA FISH CURRY

1 Tbsp coconut oil
1-in (2.5-cm) cinnamon stick
3 cloves
Seeds of 2 cardamom pods
5 black peppercorns
2 shallots, finely sliced
1 garlic clove, finely sliced
7 fresh curry leaves
1½ tsp ginger paste
¼ tsp ground turmeric
Good pinch of Himalayan salt
7 Tbsp (100 ml) water
7 Tbsp (100 ml) coconut milk
Squeeze of lime juice
3 oz (80 g) green beans, trimmed
8¾ oz (250 g) firm white flesh fish
    fillets, such as hake or haddock,
    cubed or cut into bite-size pieces

Heat the oil in a nonstick pan, add the whole spices, and cook until they release their fragrant aromas.

Add the shallots, give everything a stir for a couple of minutes, then add the garlic and curry leaves and soften for a few minutes until the shallots are translucent.

Stir in the ginger paste, turmeric, salt, and water. Bring to a boil, then lower the heat and simmer for about 7 minutes, until nicely reduced.

Add the coconut milk, squeeze in the lime juice, bring to a boil, and simmer for a couple of minutes. Add the green beans and fish fillets, just covering with the sauce. Simmer gently until the fish is cooked through, 4 to 5 minutes.

Serve with brown rice.

SERVES 2

GF   WF   DF   LF

You can cook this dish in an overproof Dutch oven before transferring it to a tagine for serving. If you prefer to cook in a tagine, however, use one with a cast-iron bottom and place it on the stove rather than in the oven. The liquid in the tagine condenses as it hits the cooler, conical-shaped lid, but if you place the tagine in the oven the lid will heat up and so won't work in quite the same way.

FALL VEGETABLE TAGINE

1 Tbsp sweet paprika
½ Tbsp ground ginger
1 tsp dried red pepper flakes
1 tsp ground coriander
1 tsp ground cumin
Seeds of 2 cardamom pods
1 garlic clove, crushed
Juice of 1 lemon
Scant ¼ cup (40 g) coconut oil, melted
2 medium carrots, cut into wedges
½ butternut squash, peeled and cut into bite-size pieces
½ small cauliflower, cut into florets
1 parsnip, peeled and cut into wedges
1 eggplant, cut into ¾-in (2-cm) cubes
14-oz (400-g) can chickpeas, drained
2 cups (500 ml) hot vegetable broth
1 Tbsp sun-dried tomato paste
Himalayan salt and black pepper

TO SERVE
Plain yogurt
Chopped fresh cilantro or Italian parsley
Gluten-free flatbreads (see page 183)

SERVES 4

Preheat the oven to 400°F (200°C).

Put the spices, garlic, lemon juice, and coconut oil (you may need to melt it over gentle heat first) in a large bowl. Add salt and pepper to taste, then mix. Add the vegetables and mix thoroughly to coat.

Heat a large ovenproof Dutch oven over medium heat, add the vegetables, and sauté for a few minutes, stirring every now and then. Add the chickpeas, broth, and sun-dried tomato paste, give everything a good stir, then cover and cook in the oven for about 30 minutes, until the vegetables are cooked and the flavors have infused. Switch off the oven, leaving the Dutch oven inside to rest for a few minutes, then transfer to a tagine for serving.

If using a tagine, reduce the amount of broth to about 1 cup (250 ml) and let simmer on the stove at the lowest possible heat for 2½ hours.

Ladle into deep bowls and serve with a spoonful of yogurt and a sprinkling of herbs on top, with flatbreads alongside.

I love this alternative twist on a classic risotto. Both wheat-free and dairy-free, this is the perfect vegetarian comfort food.

BUCKWHEAT RISOTTO WITH TAMARIND SWEET POTATO

3 Tbsp coconut oil, melted
1 medium onion, finely diced
1¼ cups (240 g) buckwheat
1⅔ cups (400 ml) hot vegetable broth
2 large sweet potatoes, chopped into bite-size pieces
1 tsp tamarind paste
Thumb-size piece of ginger, grated
1 garlic clove, crushed
2 Tbsp cashews, finely chopped
Himalayan salt

SERVES 4

Heat 1 Tbsp of the melted coconut oil in a heavy-bottom saucepan and gently sauté the onion until soft, about 8 minutes. Add the buckwheat and stir through, coating the grains with the oil. Add about ⅞ cup (200 ml) of the hot broth, bring to a boil, then gently simmer until the buckwheat is tender, adding more broth as needed.

Meanwhile, in a large mixing bowl, mix the sweet potatoes with the remaining coconut oil, tamarind paste, ginger, garlic, and a good pinch of salt. Spread out in a roasting tray and bake in the oven for 50 to 55 minutes, until crispy.

Divide the risotto between shallow bowls and top with sweet potato and chopped cashews, for a little crunch.

VARIATION
Instead of tamarind sweet potato, try ginger, chile, and cavolo nero instead. Cook the buckwheat as directed above, then heat 1 Tbsp coconut oil in a large frying pan, add thin slices of ginger, from a thumb-size piece, 1 crushed garlic clove, and 1 seeded and thinly sliced red chile with 1 tsp garam masala added after a few seconds. Cook for 30 seconds, then add 2¼ cups (200 g) shredded cavolo nero leaves, a generous pinch of salt, and a little water if necessary, to wilt, then cook for 4 to 5 minutes, stirring continuously. Add 4 tsp white wine or a splash of sherry vinegar to deglaze, then remove from the heat, cover, and set aside for a couple of minutes. Stir through the buckwheat and serve.

RAINBOW FISH PIE

4 eggs (optional)
10½ oz (300 g) sweet potatoes,
  peeled and cut into chunks
Scant ¼ cup (50 g) coconut oil
⅞ cup (200 ml) milk
2 bay leaves
1 lb 2 oz (500 g) assorted fish, such
  as cod, haddock, and salmon
  (including undyed smoked, which
  adds a lovely flavor)
3½ oz (100 g) raw shrimp, peeled
  and deveined
⅓ cup (40 g) gluten-free flour
2 tsp curry powder or ½ tsp ground
  turmeric (optional)
Bunch of fresh parsley, leaves
  minced
Himalayan salt and black pepper

SERVES 4 TO 6

This is a favorite comfort food. It may seem a real faff to cook, but I promise, it's worth the effort. Is anything more mouthwatering than homemade fish pie?

Preheat the oven to 350°F (180°C).

Place the eggs, if using, in a saucepan with cold water just covering them, then bring to a boil, turn down to a gentle simmer, and cook for 10 minutes. Drain and rinse under cold water. Shell and finely chop.

Meanwhile, put the sweet potatoes in a steamer and steam for 30 minutes, or until soft. Mash with 2 tsp of the coconut oil and salt and pepper to taste.

While the potatoes are cooking, warm the milk in a heavy-bottom saucepan. Add the bay leaves and, working in batches of similar size pieces, the fish and shrimp. Cover and cook for 6 minutes for fillets and 4 minutes for shrimp, until cooked. Remove to a dish using a slotted spoon.

When cool enough to handle, remove the skin and bones from the fish, break up any fillets into smaller pieces, and place in a large bowl. Add the chopped egg, if using. Strain the cooking liquid into a measuring cup and top off with milk if necessary to give 2 cups (500 ml).

Melt the remaining coconut oil in a pan over medium heat, add the flour and 2 cups (500 ml) cooking liquid, and cook, stirring continuously with a whisk, for 8 minutes, until the sauce starts to thicken. Continue to stir for another 2 minutes. Season to taste, add the curry powder or turmeric, if using, and the parsley, and stir to mix. Stir the sauce gently into the fish and pour the mixture into an ovenproof dish. Spread the sweet potato mash over the fish. Cook in the oven for 35 minutes. Serve with crushed garlic peas.

CRUSHED GARLIC PEAS

1 Tbsp coconut oil
1 garlic clove, crushed
500g frozen petit pois
Handful of chopped chives
Himalayan salt and black pepper

SERVES 4

This is a wonderful twist to liven up your peas, and is perfect with Rainbow Fish Pie.

Melt the coconut oil in a heavy-bottom saucepan over medium heat, then add the garlic and fry for 1 minute. Tip in the peas, stir, then cover and cook for 5 minutes, stirring occasionally.

Stir in the chives with salt and pepper to taste. Using a potato masher, crush the peas a little.

This is one of the most delicious meals imaginable. It takes a little while to make, but is well worth the effort and packed full of flavor—a definite favorite in the Lucy Bee house.

LENTIL AND VEGETABLE MOUSSAKA

2 large potatoes, scrubbed
1¼ cups (300 ml) water
¼ cup (60 g) coconut oil
10½ oz (300 g) onions, diced
7 oz (200 g) carrots, diced
1 red and 1 yellow bell pepper, diced
2 garlic cloves, crushed
1 lb 2 oz (500 g) cremini mushrooms, chopped
2 x 14-oz (400-g) cans green lentils, drained and rinsed
1 tsp ground cinnamon
1 tsp ground allspice
1 tsp freshly grated nutmeg
3 tbsp tomato paste
14-oz (400-g) can tomatoes
2 medium eggplants, sliced
Himalayan salt and black pepper

FOR THE TOPPING

2 tsp coconut oil
1 Tbsp (10 g) cornstarch
7 Tbsp (100 ml) milk
1 small egg
2 tsp Dijon mustard
Scant ¼ cup (25 g) grated cheddar
Scant ⅓ cup (25 g) grated Parmesan

SERVES 6

Preheat the oven to 350°F (180°C).

Put the potatoes and water in a pan, bring to a boil, then cover and simmer for 30 minutes, or until just cooked through. Strain and let cool before slicing into thin disks.

Melt half the coconut oil in a heavy-bottom saucepan. Add the diced vegetables, cover, and sauté until almost softened. Add the garlic and mushrooms and continue to cook until all vegetables have softened. Add the lentils, then stir in the spices, tomato paste, and chopped tomatoes. Season and simmer for 20 minutes, stirring occasionally.

Melt the remaining coconut oil and use it to brush both sides of each eggplant slice. Place on a baking sheet and cook in the oven for 5 to 10 minutes, until soft, checking regularly. You may need to brush them with a little more oil.

Spoon a layer (about a third) of the lentils and vegetables into a 14-by-10-in (35-by-25-cm) and 2¾-in (7-cm) deep ovenproof dish, add a layer of eggplant slices, followed by a layer of potato slices. Continue layering until everything is used up, which should be three layers of each.

For the topping, melt the coconut oil in a saucepan, add the cornstarch, and cook, stirring, for about 2 minutes. Pour in the milk, then bring to a boil, turn down to a simmer, and cook for 5 minutes, stirring continuously. Beat in the egg, mustard, and salt and pepper to taste, them simmer for another 2 minutes, continuing to stir.

Pour over the moussaka, sprinkle over the cheeses, and cook in the oven for 40 minutes, until bubbling. Let stand for 5 minutes before serving, with a green salad.

BROWN RICE KEDGEREE

Scant 1¼ cups (250 g) short-grain
  brown rice (or rice of your choice)
14 oz (400 g) mackerel fillets (or
  undyed smoked haddock fillets,
  or salmon)
¾ cup (175 ml) water or milk
Scant ¼ cup (50 g) coconut oil
6¼ oz (175 g) onions, minced
2 garlic cloves, crushed or minced
1 Tbsp mild curry powder
Bunch of parsley, leaves chopped
Juice of 1 lemon
4 to 6 boiled eggs, to serve

SERVES 4 TO 6

The curried flavors in this kedgeree work really well
together and make the perfect comfort food after a
long day. I always make a little too much and then eat
the leftovers the next day for breakfast or lunch.

Cook the rice according to the package directions and
set aside. Meanwhile, place the mackerel in a large frying
pan and add the water or milk to cover. Gently bring
to a boil, then reduce the heat and simmer for about
8 minutes. Drain, setting aside the liquid. When cool
enough to handle, break into flakes and remove any
skin or bones.

Heat the coconut oil in a separate pan, add the onions
and garlic, and sauté until soft, before stirring in the curry
powder. Tip in the cooked mackerel and rice, then stir
in the parsley and lemon juice and continue to warm
through over low heat.

If the mixture appears too thick, add the reserved
liquid, a little at a time, until it reaches your desired
consistency. Spoon onto plates and serve warm,
topped with a boiled egg.

BROWN RICE PASTA BAKE

Coconut oil, for greasing
10½ oz (300 g) Rizopia organic
  brown rice pasta
1¼ cups (300 g) Bolognese sauce
  (see page 180)
⅞ cup (200 g) white sauce
  (see page 178)
2 cups (150 g) grated Parmesan
Handful of chopped fresh parsley

SERVES 4

My mom makes a divine lasagna, but this is a
simplified version—it tastes every bit as wonderful
and provides all the pleasure of a lasagna, but with
a lot more ease!

Preheat the oven to 400°F (200°C). Lightly oil an
ovenproof dish.

Cook the pasta according to the package directions,
but leaving it slightly undercooked (it will cook more
when baked). Drain well.

Put the drained pasta in a large mixing bowl with the
Bolognese sauce, white sauce, 1¼ cups (100 g) of the
Parmesan, and the parsley, and stir together gently.
Transfer to the prepared dish, sprinkle with the remaining
Parmesan, and bake in the oven for 30 to 40 minutes, until
starting to brown. Remove from the oven and, if you can
resist, let it stand for 5 minutes before serving, with a
green salad.

VEGETABLES & SIDES

CAULIFLOWER AND BROCCOLI RICE

14 oz (400 g) cauliflower
7 oz (200 g) broccoli
Scant ¼ cup (40 g) coconut oil
Himalayan salt and black pepper

SERVES 2 TO 4

This is a brilliant side dish that works as a delicious, low-carb alternative to rice or pasta, with curries or meats. However, I love eating this on its own too— it makes a wonderful light lunch and is packed full of nutrients and goodness.

Cut the florets from the cauliflower and broccoli and place them in a food processor. You might need to work in two or three batches, so you don't overcrowd the bowl. Blitz to grains the size of rice.

Melt the coconut oil in a heavy-bottom frying pan over medium heat, then add in the cauliflower and broccoli and cook for 8 minutes, stirring occasionally to prevent sticking. Add salt and pepper to taste and serve.

CELERIAC FRIES

1 celeriac (celery root), about
    2¼ lb (1 kg)
2 Tbsp coconut oil, melted
1 tsp ground turmeric
Himalayan salt and black pepper

SERVES 3 TO 4

Sometimes, especially on a cozy Friday or Saturday night in, you just need a plate of fries to dig into. These celeriac fries are a great alternative to potatoes and are wonderful to snack on with dips on movie nights in with family and friends.

Preheat the oven 400°F (200°C).

Cut the celeriac into slices before peeling, using a sharp knife (potato peelers do not work on celeriac's tough skin), transferring the peeled slices to a bowl of cold water (to stop discoloration). Cut into fries, placing them back in the water as you work.

Put the coconut oil in a large bowl and tip in the (drained) fries. Stir through the turmeric with salt and pepper to taste, and mix again until each fry is coated evenly. If using you hands, beware that turmeric will dye your skin a nice yellow color.

Spread evenly over a large, heavy baking sheet, leaving plenty of space between the fries, and cook for 45 minutes, or until golden and crisp. During cooking, regularly check and turn the fries.

INDIAN-STYLE POTATOES

Scant ¼ cup (40 g) coconut oil
Thumb-size piece of ginger,
    peeled and grated
1 green chile, seeded and minced
1 tsp nigella seeds (or cumin seeds)
½ tsp ground turmeric
1 tsp ground coriander
½ tsp garam masala (see page 181)
    plus extra to finish if needed
1 lb 2 oz (500 g) cooked potatoes,
    cut into 1¼-in (3-cm) cubes
Large handful of chopped
    fresh cilantro
Himalayan salt and black pepper

SERVES 4

The spices used in this dish help to lend a real, Indian spice sensation to the potatoes. It goes well with Lamb and Spinach Korai (see page 100), and works brilliantly with chicken or salmon too.

Heat the coconut oil in a large, nonstick frying pan over medium heat, then add the ginger and cook for a minute or so. Add the chile, nigella seeds, and ground spices and cook for another minute.

Tip in the potatoes with salt and pepper to taste, and let a crust develop on the underside of the cubes before turning to brown the other sides; you may need to add a touch more oil to help with this process. Once beautifully browned and crisped all over, remove from the heat and stir in the chopped cilantro, and extra garam masala, if preferred.

ROAST POTATOES

1 lb 2 oz (500 g) Russet potatoes,
    peeled and cut into even-size
    pieces (leave small ones whole)
Scant ¼ cup (40 g) coconut oil
Himalayan salt

SERVES 4

Who would ever think that a jar of good old Lucy Bee coconut oil could be used to make the crispest, fluffiest roasties on the planet? At family dinners, we always end up with Daisy, my Nan, Aunty Pat, and Mark fighting over the crispy bits!

Preheat the oven to 400°F (200°C).
Steam the potatoes until almost falling apart, about 15 minutes. To check if they are ready, lift one out—the outer edge should be fluffy. Meanwhile, put the coconut oil in a roasting pan and place the pan in the oven to heat up. Tip the potatoes into the roasting pan and turn to coat all over in the oil. Grind a little salt over and roast in the oven for 50 to 60 minutes, until golden and crunchy, checking and turning them every now and again, and adding more oil if needed (you can even squash some of them to create more crispy edges).

POTATO AND CELERIAC MASH

8¾ oz (250 g) celeriac (celery root)
8¾ oz (250 g) potatoes
4 tsp coconut oil
Himalayan salt and black pepper

SERVES 4

I love the texture that using both potato and celeriac together brings to this mash—and the coconut oil adds a delicious creaminess. Good with casseroles and chicken dishes, and you could even try adding leftovers to homemade soups.

Using a sharp knife, peel the celeriac, then cut into chunks and place in cold water to prevent discoloration.

Peel the potatoes and cut into chunks the same size as the celeriac, so that everything cooks evenly. Place the celeriac and the potato in a steamer and cook for 30 minutes, or until tender.

Put the coconut oil in a mixing bowl, with salt and pepper to taste, add the cooked celeriac and potatoes. Use an electric hand whisk to puree to a mash (or use a potato masher, but place the ingredients in a pan to mash rather than a bowl).

SWEET POTATO MASH WITH CHIVES

2 large sweet potatoes, unpeeled
Handful of chives, minced
1 tsp coconut oil
Himalayan salt and black pepper

SERVES 2

At the end of a long, grueling day, there's nothing better than putting my feet up and digging in to a huge bowlful of this mash. Try adding dried red pepper flakes or a teaspoon of one of the flavored oils on pages 176 to 177.

Preheat the oven to 350°F (180°C). Bake the sweet potatoes for 40 minutes, until soft. Remove and set aside to cool for 5 minutes, then cut each in half and, using a spoon, scoop the cooked insides into a bowl.

Add the chives and coconut oil and mash until you reach your desired texture (I like it really smooth). Season well before serving.

1¼ lb (600 g) sweet potatoes,
    scrubbed and cut into wedges
2 Tbsp coconut oil, melted
1 tsp hot sweet smoked paprika

SERVES 4

These wonderful, crisp wedges go well with just
about any dish, or as a side with Greek yogurt and
garlic. I sometimes sprinkle nigella seeds over before
cooking, which adds a great twist and packs a real
flavor punch.

Preheat the oven to 350°F (180°C).
    Toss the sweet potato wedges in the melted coconut
oil and sprinkle over the paprika. Tip into a roasting
pan or baking sheet and roast in the oven for 50 to
55 minutes, until crispy and delicious.

3 sweet potatoes, unpeeled
1 Tbsp coconut oil, melted
1 level tsp mild or hot paprika
    (or sweet chili)

TOPPING SUGGESTIONS
- 1 avocado, crushed and mixed
  with the juice of ½ lime and
  1 tsp dried red pepper flakes
- Greek yogurt mixed with
  crushed garlic, ½ cucumber, and
  chopped chives
- 4 chopped tomatoes, mixed with
  1 chopped red onion and a
  handful of chopped fresh parsley
- Mozzarella, torn, Parmesan,
  grated, or feta, crumbled

SERVES 2

This is one of those recipes that turns unhealthy
foods healthy. Maybe just don't add the cheese!

Preheat the oven to 350°F (180°C).
    Rinse the potatoes well, then slice into very thin, even
disks, about 2mm (¹⁄₁₆ in) (the thinner the better). Place in
a mixing bowl with the melted coconut oil and paprika
and turn the disks until evenly coated. Spread them
out evenly on a large baking sheet, being careful not to
overlap or overcrowd them.
    Cook in the oven for 35 minutes, turning every now
and again so that they crisp evenly. Reduce the oven
temperature to 275°F (140°C) and, if serving with cheese,
sprinkle this over at this point. Cook for another
6 minutes, then remove from the oven and let cool
slightly before adding your chosen toppings.

Vegetables that used to be steamed in our house are often now roasted. Roasting really adds another dimension, in Brussels sprouts, for example, bringing out a deliciously nutty and sweet flavor. For a quick lunch, sprinkle grated cheese over the roasted cauliflower and replace in the oven for 5 minutes to melt the cheese.

ROASTED VEGETABLES

GF WF DF LF V

ASPARAGUS

1 lb 2 oz (500 g) asparagus spears,
  woody ends broken off
4 tsp coconut oil, melted
Balsamic vinegar (optional, drizzle on
  once cooked)

BROCCOLI WITH GARLIC

1 lb 2 oz (500 g) broccoli, cut into
  even-size florets
2 garlic cloves, crushed
4 tsp coconut oil, melted

CAULIFLOWER WITH TURMERIC

1 lb 2 oz (500 g) cauliflower, cut into
  even-size florets
2 tsp turmeric or curry powder
  (see page 181 for homemade)
4 tsp coconut oil, melted

BRUSSELS SPROUTS

4 tsp coconut oil
1 lb 2 oz (500 g) Brussels sprouts,
  outer leaves removed

SERVES 2

Preheat the oven to 350°F (180°C).

For the asparagus, broccoli, and cauliflower, toss the ingredients together well, season with Himalayan salt and ground black pepper, and roast in a single layer on a baking sheet for about 15 minutes, until cooked to your liking (the edges of the broccoli should be slightly brown and crispy).

For the Brussels sprouts, heat the coconut oil on a baking sheet in the oven, then remove and add the sprouts. Coat well, season, and roast for about 45 minutes until browned, reducing the oven temperature a little after 15 minutes.

SOUPS & SALADS

It's easy to see why soups are so popular in the cold winter months—comforting, incredibly nourishing, and satisfying, and quick and easy to make. I adore all kinds of soups but have a particular soft spot for this beet one. Not only does its color make it look beautiful, it's also full of nutrients and minerals, including potassium, magnesium, and iron, as well as antioxidants and soluble fiber.

BEET SOUP

1 Tbsp coconut oil,
    plus extra to finish
1 onion, chopped
2 garlic cloves, chopped
1 lb 10 oz (750 g) cooked beet,
    chopped (or start from raw)
2 cups (500 ml) hot vegetable broth
1 Tbsp freshly grated horseradish
    or 2 Tbsp good-quality
    horseradish sauce from a
    jar (optional)

TO SERVE
Greek yogurt
Chopped chives

SERVES 4

Melt the coconut oil in a pan, add the onion and garlic, and cook over medium heat for a few minutes until translucent. Add the beet and broth and simmer, covered, for 20 minutes.

Pour into a blender and blitz until smooth. Tip back into the saucepan and stir in the horseradish, if using, and then a little extra coconut oil for a lovely, creamy finish. Pour into bowls and top with a dollop of yogurt and some chopped chives.

TIP If cooking the beet from raw, leave them unpeeled and wash thoroughly. Place in a large pan of water, bring to a boil, and then simmer for 30 to 60 minutes, depending on the size of the beet, until soft when pierced with a sharp knife. Let cool, then peel.

While many people think of soup as a winter comfort, this refreshing blend is delicious all year round. I love its unique coconut water twist, which makes the soup even more nourishing and hydrating. I sometimes sprinkle over dried shredded coconut for extra sweetness, and a spoonful of flavored oil (see pages 176 to 177) adds flavor. All in all, this is the perfect meal to put a spring in your step and fight any weekday blues.

CARROT AND COCONUT SOUP

1 Tbsp coconut oil
14 oz (400 g) carrots, chopped
½ butternut squash, peeled, seeded, and chopped
1 white onion, chopped
1-in (2.5-cm) piece of ginger, peeled and grated
2 garlic cloves, chopped
1 green chile, seeded and sliced
¼ tsp ground cumin
¼ tsp ground coriander
¼ tsp ground turmeric
3 cups (750 ml) hot vegetable broth
2 cups (500 ml) coconut water
1 Tbsp lime juice
Roasted pumpkin seeds or
    Greek yogurt, to garnish (optional)

Melt the coconut oil in a pan over gentle heat, then add the carrots, squash, and onion, and cook until golden and slightly softened. Add the ginger, garlic, and chile, and cook for another 5 minutes.

Stir in the spices, then pour in the broth, and simmer for 15 to 20 minutes, until the vegetables are soft. Tip into a blender and blitz until smooth.

Pour the soup back into the pan and add enough coconut water to bring it to your desired consistency. Gently heat, then simmer for 2 to 3 minutes. Ladle into bowls, squeeze over the lime juice, and top with pumpkin seeds or yogurt, if using.

SERVES 4

GF WF LF VEG

My friend Hannah's adaptation of a classic tomato soup is suitable for anyone wanting a dairy-free option. Serve with Flaxseed Bread with Anchovy and Rosemary (see page 183) and to spice things up, stir in a teaspoon of Spicy Coconut Oil Harissa (see page 177).

MY FAVORITE TOMATO SOUP

1 Tbsp coconut oil
2 celery stalks, chopped
2 carrots, peeled and chopped
1 garlic clove, chopped
1 large onion, chopped
1 cup (250 ml) hot vegetable broth
2 x 14-oz (400-g) cans tomatoes
A few fresh basil leaves or 2 tsp dried
2 tsp tomato paste
1 x 5½-oz (160-ml) can coconut
    cream (or use ⅞ cup (200 ml)
    coconut milk)
Himalayan salt and black pepper

SERVES 4

GF WF DF LF V

Melt the coconut oil in a heavy-bottom saucepan, add the celery, carrots, garlic, and onion and gently sauté for 5 to 10 minutes, until soft.

Add the broth and stir for a few minutes, then tip in the chopped tomatoes and basil, if using dried, then mix in the tomato paste and coconut cream. Bring to a boil, cover, then simmer for about 30 minutes.

Tip into a blender and blitz until smooth and creamy, then season to taste, ladle into bowls, and serve, with fresh basil leaves on top, if using.

This is my twist on a good old classic soup, with cannellini beans added for goodness and creaminess. It also freezes well, so this deliciously warming soup is ideal for making in bulk.

LEEK AND SWEET POTATO SOUP

1 Tbsp coconut oil
12¼ oz (350 g) leeks, sliced
2 garlic cloves, chopped
1 lb 2 oz (500 g) sweet potatoes, peeled and chopped
1 tsp dried rosemary
4½ cups (1 liter) hot vegetable broth
14-oz (400-g) can cannellini beans, well rinsed
Handful of chopped chives
Himalayan salt and black pepper

SERVES 4 TO 6

Heat the coconut oil in a heavy-bottom saucepan, add the leeks and garlic, cover, and sweat for 5 minutes.

Add the sweet potatoes, rosemary, and broth, then season well with salt and pepper. Bring to a boil, cover, and simmer for 15 minutes, or until the potatoes have softened.

Add the beans and heat everything together for a few minutes, then pour into a blender and blitz until smooth. Stir in the chopped chives before spooning into bowls to serve.

This is one of my absolute favorite meals as it's so full of flavor. I like to make big batches of this to freeze and reheat as a quick meal in the winter months, when nothing but a huge bowl of comforting soup will do.

LENTIL SOUP

2 Tbsp coconut oil
1 large onion, chopped
2 garlic cloves, chopped
1 thumb-size piece of ginger,
    peeled and chopped
1¼ cups (250 g) red lentils
3 cups (750 ml) hot vegetable broth
Juice of ½ lemon
Himalayan salt and black pepper

SERVES 4 TO 6

Heat the coconut oil in a saucepan, add the onion, garlic, and ginger and sauté for about 5 minutes, or until the onions start to color.

Add the lentils and broth, then bring to a boil, stirring occasionally to prevent the lentils from catching. Reduce the heat to low, cover, and cook for 15 to 20 minutes.

Add the lemon juice, then pour into a blender and blitz until smooth. Season to taste, ladle into bowls, and serve.

VARIATIONS
Although this soup tastes great smooth, it's also nice with just half blended and half left as it is, to give it some texture. If you want an extra kick of flavor, add a teaspoon of turmeric, or serve with sautéed sliced garlic sprinkled over the top.

ROASTED CITRUS SALAD

1 orange, sliced into thin circles
1 lemon, sliced into thin circles
1 tsp coconut oil, melted
½ small red onion, thinly sliced
½ fennel, shaved, plus a handful
    of fronds, to serve
4¼ oz (120 g) corn salad
2 avocados, peeled and sliced
Himalayan salt

SERVES 4

**When you roast citrus fruits at a high temperature
they caramelize, giving a lovely texture and depth
of flavor to a salad.**

Preheat the oven to 425°F (220°C).
    In a large mixing bowl, toss the orange and lemon
slices with the melted coconut oil.
    Line a roasting tray with parchment paper and tip
the citrus slices onto the tray. Spread out in a single
layer and roast in the oven for 10 to 15 minutes, tossing
occasionally, until caramelized. Let cool.
    Soak the red onion slices in iced water for a few
minutes (to reduce their harshness), then drain and put
into a mixing bowl. Add the cooled citrus slices, fennel
shavings, and corn salad and toss everything together,
along with a pinch of salt and the remaining melted
coconut oil.
    Add the avocado and toss very gently again, to bring
everything together, then transfer to a serving bowl.
Sprinkle over the fennel fronds and serve.

ROASTED EGGPLANT SALAD WITH LEMON SAFFRON YOGURT

2 eggplants, cut into thick
    1¼-in (3-cm) circles
2 Tbsp coconut oil,
    melted
Mixed radishes, finely sliced
Handful of microherbs or
    baby leaves
Himalayan salt

FOR THE DRESSING
3 saffron threads
7 Tbsp (100 ml) plain yogurt
Finely grated zest and juice of
    1 lemon

SERVES 4

**The robust flavors in this salad make it the perfect
accompaniment to barbecued meats.**

Preheat the oven to 425°F (220°C).
    In a large bowl, toss the eggplant circles in the
coconut oil and ½ tsp salt. Spread out on a baking
sheet and bake for 15 to 20 minutes, until a deep golden
color. Meanwhile, place the saffron threads in 3 Tbsp
(45 ml) hot water and let infuse for 20 minutes. To make
the dressing, mix together the saffron-infused water,
yogurt, lemon zest and juice, with salt to taste.
    Place the eggplant circles on a platter, spoon over
a generous amount of dressing, and sprinkle over the
radish slices and microherbs or baby leaves.

My brother isn't a massive fan of salads, but as soon as there's halloumi in sight, his plate will be licked clean! I too love halloumi, in all manner of dishes, as I find that its slightly salty taste really lifts ingredients. Drizzled with a fresh lemon and avocado-oil dressing, this converts even the most stubborn of salad haters.

HALLOUMI SALAD

7¾ oz (225 g) halloumi
1 tsp coconut oil
Handful of chopped fresh parsley

FOR THE DRESSING
2 Tbsp lemon juice
2 Tbsp olive oil
2 Tbsp avocado oil
1 tsp Dijon mustard
4 tsp agave nectar
1 tsp cashew butter
Heaping 1 tsp capers, chopped
Ground black pepper, to taste

TO SERVE
2 Tbsp pine nuts
3½ oz (100 g) arugula
14 cherry tomatoes, halved
½ cucumber, seeded and
    chopped into quarters
6 scallions, minced
14 green or black olives

SERVES 2

To make the dressing, place all the ingredients in a bottle or recycled Lucy Bee jar and shake until combined. Set aside.

Pat the halloumi dry using paper towels, then cut into ¾-in (2-cm) slices. Melt the coconut oil in a frying pan over medium heat. When hot, add the halloumi slices and cook for about 1 minute on each side, until lightly browned. Remove and set aside, then add the pine nuts for serving to the pan, lightly toast, and set aside.

Arrange the salad ingredients on plates and place the halloumi slices on top. Pour the dressing over (you may have too much, in which case store in an airtight container in the refrigerator for up to 5 days), then sprinkle over the parsley and toasted pine nuts and serve immediately.

Kale is a nutritious superfood, which makes the perfect base for any salad. Combine with juicy figs and different colored heritage beets, this salad is almost too pretty to eat.

BABY KALE WITH HERITAGE BEETS, FIGS, AND RICOTTA

4 heritage beets, a mixture of colors
2 Tbsp coconut oil, melted
4 ripe figs, cut into quarters
4¼ oz (120 g) baby kale
   (or watercress)
Scant 1 cup (200 g) ricotta
Himalayan salt and black pepper

FOR THE DRESSING
2 Tbsp avocado oil
1 Tbsp pomegranate molasses
1 Tbsp cider vinegar

SERVES 4

Preheat the oven to 350°F (180°C).
   Wash the beets to remove any dirt. Coat the beets in the melted coconut oil and arrange on a roasting tray. Roast in the oven for 45 minutes, until the beets feel tender when pierced with a skewer. Set aside to cool.
   Once cool, slice the beets into thin circles. Place the beets, figs, and kale in a large serving bowl. Lightly dress the salad and taste for seasoning. Add small spoonfuls of ricotta before serving.

DESSERTS

I love making this at the weekend as it feels as though you're indulging in a decadent ice-cream sundae. However, it's dairy-free and about as healthy as it comes—there's the amazing health benefits you get from the potassium found in the bananas, while the gentle sweetness from the cinnamon curbs sugar cravings. The lucuma powder makes it a little sweeter and adds a butterscotch-like flavor to the dish.

BANANA AND STRAWBERRY "ICE CREAM"

4 strawberries, for dipping

FOR THE CHOCOLATE SAUCE
2 tsp raw cacao or unsweetened
   cocoa powder
2 tsp coconut oil
1 tsp almond milk

FOR THE ICE CREAM
2 medium ripe bananas,
   sliced and frozen
2 strawberries
1 tsp ground cinnamon
1 tsp lucuma powder (optional)
1/3 cup (80 ml) almond milk

SERVES 2

To make the chocolate sauce, put the ingredients in a small pan and gently melt, stirring until smooth and taking care it doesn't burn. Dip the four strawberries into the chocolate sauce and transfer to the refrigerator to set. Set aside any remaining chocolate sauce, for serving.

Put the frozen bananas into a blender with the strawberries, cinnamon, and lucuma, if using. With the motor running, slowly pour in the almond milk and blend until it reaches an ice cream-like texture. You may need to stop the blender and give it a stir with a spoon until it reaches the correct, thick consistency.

Spoon into chilled bowls (to stop it melting too quickly), top with the dipped strawberries, and drizzle over any remaining chocolate sauce.

Few things are more British than a spot of blackberry picking in the late summer—and this dessert is worth saving them for. On cooking, the mixture separates, resulting in a light, almost soufflé-like sponge sitting atop a lemon and blackberry sauce.

BLACKBERRY AND LEMON SAUCE PUDDING

Scant ¼ cup (50 g) coconut oil, melted, plus extra for greasing
1¼ cups (175 g) blackberries
¾ cup (150 g) superfine sugar
Finely grated zest of 3 unwaxed lemons, and 7 Tbsp (100 ml) juice
3 large eggs, separated
1¼ cups (300 ml) milk
Scant ½ cup (50 g) gluten-free all-purpose flour, sifted
¼ tsp gluten-free baking powder
Powdered sugar, for dusting

SERVES 6 TO 8

GF   WF   VEG

Preheat the oven to 350°F (180°C). Lightly grease a 1.3-quart (1.5-liter) ovenproof dish with coconut oil.

Spread the blackberries evenly over the bottom of the dish and set aside. Put the coconut oil, sugar, and lemon zest in a bowl and, using an electric whisk, whisk until fluffy. Gradually add the egg yolks, lemon juice, and milk, whisking all the time, until well combined.

Sift the flour and baking powder together, then add this to the mixture and whisk well until you have a smooth batter, then set aside.

Whisk the egg whites to a stiff, but not dry, peak. Stir 1 Tbsp of the whisked egg whites into the mixture, to loosen, then fold in the remaining whites in two batches, taking care to keep it aerated and not to overwork. Pour this batter into the prepared dish over the blackberries.

Bake in the middle of the oven for 40 to 45 minutes, or until the top is golden brown and springs back when gently touched. Remove from the oven and serve hot, with a light dusting of powdered sugar, and a dollop of crème fraîche, if desired.

BLUEBERRY CLAFOUTIS

4 tsp coconut oil, melted
4 large eggs
⅛ cup (30 g) stevia or ¼ cup +
    2 Tbsp (75 g) superfine sugar
½ cup + 2 Tbsp (75 g) gluten-free
    all-purpose flour
½ tsp gluten-free baking powder
1¼ cups (300 ml) almond milk
1 cup (150 g) blueberries
Powdered sugar, for dusting

SERVES 6 TO 8

Blueberries—I just can't seem to leave them
alone and would eat them all day if I could!
This mouthwatering clafoutis is the perfect dessert
to dish up on a warm spring or summer's day.

Preheat the oven to 400°F (200°C). Lightly grease a
shallow 1.3-quart (1.5-liter) baking dish with coconut oil.

Put the eggs and stevia or sugar into a mixing bowl and
beat until combined, light, and frothy. Sift the flour and
baking powder together, then beat into the egg mixture
until well incorporated.

Gradually pour in the melted coconut oil and
continue to beat until well blended. Slowly add the milk,
continuing to beat to ensure it's mixed well.

Pour this batter into the prepared dish and sprinkle
over the blueberries. Bake in the middle of the oven for
35 to 40 minutes, or until well-risen and golden brown.
Remove from the oven, dust with powdered sugar, and
serve, with a little crème fraîche, if desired.

RAW CHOCOLATE CHEESECAKE

FOR THE BASE
2 cups (225 g) pecans
¼ cup (25 g) raw cacao powder
4 Tbsp (60 ml) raw agave nectar
Scant ¼ cup (50 g) coconut oil
Scant ¼ cup (50 g) peanut butter
Pinch of Himalayan salt

FOR THE FILLING
1¼ cups (150 g) cashews, soaked in
    cold water for 4 hours (or for
    2 hours in hot if short of time)
1 ripe avocado
⅓ cup (30 g) raw cacao powder
7 Tbsp (100 ml) coconut milk
¼ cup (50 g) coconut oil, melted
2 Tbsp raw agave nectar

SERVES 8 TO 12

Who doesn't love a cheesecake? Especially when it's
raw, dairy-free, and packed with nutrients. Serve this
to friends and they'll never know it's good for them.

Line an 8-in (20-cm) round springform cake pan with
parchment paper.

To make the base, put all ingredients into a blender
or food processor and blitz until crumbly. Tip the
mixture into the lined cake pan, spread it out evenly
and press down firmly. Place in the freezer while you
make the filling.

Drain the cashews and blitz in a food processor until
they resemble cashew butter. Add the remaining filling
ingredients and whiz until smooth.

Remove the base from the freezer and spread the filling
over the top. Place back in the freezer for at least 2 hours,
removing 10 minutes before serving, with berries and
crème fraîche, if desired. Store in the freezer.

Raspberries are one of those fruits that we always seem to have an abundance of come early summer, and this cake is a delicious way to use up any berries you have leftover from picking. Perfect for summer afternoon teas or picnics.

CHOCOLATE SPONGE WITH RASPBERRIES

7 Tbsp (100 g) coconut oil, melted
4 large eggs, separated
½ cup (120 ml) warm water
1 tsp vanilla extract
Scant ⅔ cup (120 g) stevia
1 cup (130 g) gluten-free
   all-purpose flour
Heaping 2 Tbsp unsweetened
   cocoa powder
¼ tsp xanthan gum
3 tsp gluten-free baking powder

FOR THE TOPPING
1 cup (250 g) crème fraîche
1 Tbsp runny honey
3¼ cups (400 g) fresh raspberries

SERVES 8

Preheat the oven to 350°F (180°C). Lightly grease an 8-in (20-cm) round springform cake pan and line with parchment paper.

Place the egg yolks in a mixing bowl and beat using an electric whisk. While still whisking, slowly pour in the coconut oil, warm water, and vanilla and continue until well combined.

Sift together the stevia, flour, cocoa powder, xanthan gum, and 2 tsp of the baking powder. Gently fold the dry ingredients into the egg yolk mixture.

In a separate bowl, whisk the egg whites with the remaining baking powder until stiff. Carefully fold the egg whites into the cake batter, then pour into the prepared pan. Bake in the oven for 25 to 30 minutes, or until a skewer comes out clean and the sponge springs back to the touch. Remove from the oven and let cool in the pan for 5 minutes, before turning out onto a wire rack to cool completely.

Mix the crème fraîche with the honey and spread over the top of the cooled cake, then decorate with the raspberries.

Rhubarb is incredibly easy to grow and its tart flavor always works so well in steamed sponge desserts. This is a proper British dessert and takes me right back to childhood.

STEAMED ORANGE DESSERTS WITH POACHED RHUBARB

¼ cup (60 g) coconut oil, melted
7 oz (200 g) rhubarb, cut into ¾-in (2-cm) pieces
9 Tbsp agave nectar
3 large eggs
½ cup (100 g) stevia or ½ cup + 2 Tbsp (125 g) superfine sugar
Finely grated zest and juice of 3 oranges
1½ cups (175 g) all-purpose flour
1½ tsp gluten-free baking powder
Pinch of xanthan gum

SERVES 6

GF WF DF LF VEG

TIP If you don't have a steamer, use a large saucepan instead. Place a dinner plate upside down on the bottom of the pan, then put the ovenproof bowls on top of the plate. Fill the saucepan with enough cold water to cover the bottom one-third of the molds. Bring to a boil, cover with a lid, then steam until cooked.

Have a steamer ready on top of the stove. Lightly grease six 5-oz (150-ml) ovenproof bowls with a little coconut oil.

Place half the rhubarb into the bowls, tightly lining the bottoms. Pour 1 Tbsp of the agave nectar into each bowl, then set aside.

Put the eggs in a bowl with the stevia or sugar and whisk on high speed, using an electric mixer, until light and creamy, 5 to 10 minutes. Beat in the melted coconut oil and orange zest. Sift the flour, baking powder, and xanthan gum together and carefully fold this into the egg mixture, ensuring that it is well combined.

Divide the batter evenly between the ovenproof dishes, making sure they are not more than three-quarters full. Cover each bowl with a small square of foil and fold under the rim of the bowls to seal. Place in the steamer and steam for 20 to 25 minutes, or until the sponge has risen and just springs back to the touch.

Meanwhile, place the remaining rhubarb in a saucepan with the orange juice and remaining agave nectar. Lightly poach for 5 to 10 minutes, until the rhubarb is just cooked and keeping its shape, taking care not to overcook it.

Carefully remove the desserts from the steamer and remove the foil tops. Run a knife around the edges to loosen and turn them onto plates. Serve at once, with the warm poached rhubarb and some crème fraîche, if desired, and some of the rhubarb cooking juices drizzled over.

COCONUT RICE PUDDING WITH FRESH MANGO AND TOASTED COCONUT

1 Tbsp coconut oil
⅓ cup (80 g) short-grain rice
1 x 14-oz (400-ml) can coconut milk
1⅔ cups (400 ml) water
4 tsp stevia
1 vanilla bean, split lengthwise
1 mango, cut into small slices
¼ cup (20 g) coconut flakes, toasted

SERVES 4

Coconut works so well with tropical fruits and flavors. This wonderfully creamy, sweet, and nourishing dish is a twist on the classic rice pudding. It makes the perfect breakfast, or a luxurious dessert when nothing but a sweet treat will do.

Heat the coconut oil in a large saucepan until hot, then add the rice and stir for about 2 minutes, until lightly toasted and coated with oil, but not browned.

Pour in the coconut milk, water, and stevia, and stir. Bring to a boil, then reduce to a simmer. Add the vanilla bean and simmer for 35 to 40 minutes, until cooked, stirring to ensure it doesn't catch on the bottom of the saucepan. Pour into individual bowls, top with the mango slices and toasted coconut flakes, and serve.

VARIATIONS
This works well with raspberries and slivered almonds, or blackberries and apple—try what takes your fancy!

BROWN RICE PUDDING WITH RAW FRUIT PUREE

2 Tbsp coconut oil
¼ cup (50 g) coconut sugar or
   brown sugar
½ cup (100 g) brown rice
2 cups (500 ml) milk or coconut milk
1 vanilla bean, split lengthwise
Mixed frozen or fresh berries

SERVES 4

Although I try to cut back on sugar, this creamy rice pudding is a special treat—everything in moderation! The whole grain brown rice and whole milk makes this a nutritious dessert.

Preheat the oven to 275°F (140°C).

Over medium heat, melt the coconut oil in an ovenproof pan or Dutch oven. Add the sugar and stir for a few moments until it goes syrupy, then tip in the brown rice. Stir, add the milk, stirring constantly to avoid catching. Be careful as it will bubble and froth up!

Add the vanilla bean, then cover and cook in the oven for 2 hours. Remove the vanilla bean, scraping the seeds into the rice, then give everything a good stir.

Gently blitz the berries in a blender, or mash them with a fork. Serve the rice pudding in bowls with a dollop of fruit puree in the center of each.

Lucy Bee coconut oil works so well in place of butter in crumble toppings—I use this simple mix for loads of different fruit fillings and never get tired of it. Either stick to this recipe or try using whatever comes to hand, maybe a mixture of cornmeal and buckwheat flour instead of all-purpose flour, or add dried shredded coconut. My Healthy Seed Mix (see page 182) works a treat too! Any seasonal fruit works in place of the raspberries.

RASPBERRY, CACAO NIB, AND COCONUT OIL CRUMBLE

8 cups (450 g) fresh raspberries
1/3 cup (80 g) chilled coconut oil, cut into small pieces
2/3 cup (80 g) gluten-free all-purpose flour
1/3 cup (80 g) coconut sugar or soft brown sugar
Scant 1 cup (80 g) ground almonds
2 Tbsp cacao nibs

SERVES 4

GF | WF | DF | LF | V

Preheat the oven to 350°F (180°C).

Layer the raspberries into an ovenproof dish measuring approximately 8 in (20 cm) in diameter.

Put the coconut oil pieces, flour, sugar, and ground almonds in a food processor and blitz to a granular consistency, taking care not to overprocess to a dough. Add the cacao nibs and mix them in quickly using a spoon.

Spoon the crumble mixture over the raspberries and bake in the oven for 20 minutes, until the crumble is colored and the raspberries start to bubble through. Serve hot, with a spoonful of crème fraîche, if desired.

Gluten-free pie dough is quite tricky to make and roll out, so I have to admit I sometimes get help with that bit! However, it tastes so delicious that it's most definitely worth the patience—perfect for a Friday or Saturday night treat, especially served with Banana and Strawberry "Ice Cream" (see page 140).

STRAWBERRY AND HAZELNUT TART

FOR THE PIE DOUGH
½ cup (100 g) coconut oil
1⅔ cups (200 g) all-purpose flour
⅓ cup (45 g) powdered sugar
¼ tsp xanthan gum
¼ cup (30 g) roasted chopped hazelnuts
1 egg yolk
2 to 4 Tbsp cold water

FOR THE FILLING
7 Tbsp (100 ml) Greek yogurt
2 cups (500 ml) crème fraîche
2 Tbsp honey
2¾ cups (400 g) strawberries

SERVES 6 TO 8

Preheat the oven to 400°F (200°C). Lightly grease a 9-in (23-cm), loose-bottomed fluted tart pan.

To make the pie dough, put the flour, powdered sugar, xanthan gum, and coconut oil in a food processor and process until the mixture resembles bread crumbs. Add the chopped hazelnuts, egg yolk, and 2 Tbsp of cold water and mix again until the mixture comes together, adding more water if necessary. Remove and shape the dough into a circle, then wrap in plastic wrap and let rest for 15 minutes in the refigerator.

Roll out the dough between two sheets of plastic wrap until quite thin (about ⅛ in/3 mm thick) and big enough to line the tart pan. Gently peel off the top sheet of plastic wrap and carefully invert the dough into the pan. Remove the second sheet of plastic wrap. If the dough crumbles or tears, use your fingers to mold it into the gaps, as it's quite pliable. Neaten off the top edge of the dough and chill in the freezer for 5 minutes.

Remove from the freezer, use a fork to prick the bottom in a few places, line with parchment paper, and fill with pie weights. Bake blind for 10 to 15 minutes, or until the dough is just beginning to color. Remove the pie weights and parchment and return to the oven for another 5 minutes, until golden and cooked. Let cool.

Unmold the cold pastry shell from the pan and place on a serving plate. Put the yogurt, crème fraîche, and honey in a bowl and mix well together. Pour into the cooked pastry shell, smoothing over the top. Cut the strawberries into eighths and arrange in circles to decorate.

CAKES & COOKIES

This cake makes the most amazing centerpiece for afternoon teas. It looks really impressive when set on a cake stand—so much so that I bet your friends or family won't have a clue that it's so healthy. The summer berries contrast wonderfully with the rich chocolate sponge and creamy frosting.

DARK CHOCOLATE CAKE WITH DAIRY-FREE FROSTING

¼ cup (60 g) coconut oil, melted
3⅛ cups (300 g) almond flour
¼ cup (60 g) coconut sugar
1 Tbsp raw cacao powder
4 Tbsp coconut flour
2 tsp baking soda
4 large eggs
1 cup (240 ml) almond milk
3½ oz (100 g) semisweet chocolate
    (at least 70% cocoa solids), melted
1 Tbsp vanilla extract
Fresh raspberries, blackberries, and
    cape gooseberries, to decorate

FOR THE FROSTING

2 cups (250 g) cashews, soaked in
    cold water overnight, then drained
1 Tbsp lucuma powder
4 Tbsp powdered sugar, or to taste
4 Tbsp coconut oil, melted
2 Tbsp almond milk
1 Tbsp vanilla extract

SERVES 8

Preheat the oven to 350°F (180°C). Lightly grease two 8-in (20-cm) round springform cake pans and line with parchment paper.

In a large bowl, mix together the almond flour, coconut sugar, cacao powder, coconut flour, and baking soda.

In a separate bowl, and using an electric whisk, whisk together the coconut oil, eggs, almond milk, melted chocolate, and vanilla until smooth and frothy.

Gently fold the dry ingredients into the wet until combined. Take care not to let too much air out of the batter—stop as soon as the dry ingredients are just folded through. Divide between the two prepared cake pans. Bake in the oven for 20 to 25 minutes, or until a skewer comes out clean. Leave in the cake pans for 5 minutes before turning out onto a wire rack to cool completely.

Blitz the frosting ingredients together until smooth. Taste and add more powdered sugar or milk if necessary. Spread half the frosting over one of the cooled cakes, then sprinkle over half the raspberries. Place the second cake on top and spread with the remaining frosting. Top with more berries and then finish off with cape gooseberries. Enjoy, with a spoonful of crème fraîche if desired.

This is a really impressive-looking dessert to serve up to family or friends on a hot summer's day. The pineapple and passion fruit make this classic completely irresistible. Simply perfect for those summer barbecues and get-togethers.

PINEAPPLE AND PASSION FRUIT ROULADE

FOR THE ROULADE

1 Tbsp coconut oil, melted
4 large eggs
Heaping ¼ cup (55 g) stevia
1 tsp vanilla extract
⅔ cup (80 g) gluten-free
   all-purpose flour
1 tsp gluten-free baking powder
Pinch of xanthan gum
Powdered sugar, for dusting
Edible flowers, such as violas or
   nasturtiums, to decorate

FOR THE FILLING

⅝ cup (150 ml) Greek yogurt
⅝ cup (150 ml) crème fraîche
4 tsp agave nectar
3 passion fruit
4¼ oz (125 g) fresh pineapple,
   cut into very small chunks

SERVES 6 TO 8

GF   WF   VEG

Preheat the oven to 350°C (180°C). Lightly grease a 13½-by-9-in (34-by-23-cm) jelly roll pan or shallow baking sheet and line with parchment paper.

Place the eggs and stevia in a bowl and whisk for 5 to 10 minutes on high speed using an electric mixer until creamy, light, and almost doubled in volume. Beal in the melted coconut oil and vanilla extract.

Sift the flour, baking powder, and xanthan gum together, then gently fold into the egg mixture, until combined. Take care not to let too much air out of the batter—stop as soon as the dry ingredients are just folded through. Pour into the prepared pan and bake in the middle of the oven for 12 to 15 minutes, or until the sponge springs back to the touch.

Let cool slightly in the pan. Place a flat sheet of parchment paper on the counter, lightly dusted with powdered sugar. Turn out the warm roulade onto the parchment and start to roll from the narrower end of the cake (the paper will remain inside) until you have a jelly roll. Let cool completely.

Once completely cold, unroll the roulade and discard the parchment. Mix together the yogurt, crème fraîche, and agave nectar. Scoop out the seeds and pulp from the passion fruit and fold into the yogurt mixture. Spread the fruity yogurt over the roulade and sprinkle over the pineapple chunks, setting some aside for decoration.

Carefully roll up the roulade and place on a serving dish. Sprinkle the remaining pineapple chunks over the top of the roulade and dust with powdered sugar. Decorate with edible flowers, such as violas and nasturtiums.

CAKES & COOKIES

I've recently started using cornmeal more and more and I love its versatility—it tastes great in savory meals (cornmeal fries just have to be tried!) and, as you can see here, it also works brilliantly with sweet ingredients too. Here it adds a lovely, crunchy texture. The perfect bake to serve with a cup of green tea on rainy afternoons, or as a dessert, with ice cream or crème fraîche.

CORNMEAL AND LEMON CAKE

⅓ cup (75 g) superfine sugar
⅔ cup (150 g) coconut oil, softened
4 large eggs
1 Tbsp gluten-free baking powder
¾ cup (100 g) fine cornmeal
2¼ cups (200 g) ground almonds
Finely grated zest of 2 unwaxed
    lemons, and 4 tsp juice
Fresh sprigs of edible flowers,
    to decorate

FOR THE SUGAR SYRUP
Juice of 1 lemon
⅔ cup (75 g) powdered sugar

SERVES 6 TO 8

GF | WF | DF | LF | VEG

Preheat the oven to 350°F (180°C). Line an 8-in (20-cm) round springform cake pan with parchment paper.

Using an electric hand whisk, beat the sugar and coconut oil together until smooth, then add the eggs and beat until combined.

Stir in the baking powder, cornmeal, ground almonds, lemon zest and juice, then pour the batter into the prepared cake pan. Bake in the oven for 35 to 40 minutes, or until a skewer comes out clean.

Meanwhile, put the lemon juice and powdered sugar for the sugar syrup in a small saucepan and gently warm until the syrup turns clear. Remove from the heat and set aside.

When the cake comes out of the oven, prick it all over with a fork and then pour the syrup over. Let cool completely in the cake pan before turning out onto a serving plate. Top with more sugar syrup and then finish off with sprigs of edible flowers, such as rosemary or lavender.

RAW BROWNIES

½ cup (60 g) pecans
½ cup (60 g) hazelnuts
5 oz (140 g) Medjool dates, pitted
   and chopped
5 Tbsp raw cacao powder
2 Tbsp coconut oil, melted
3 Tbsp dried shredded coconut
3 Tbsp runny honey or maple syrup
1 tsp vanilla extract
Pinch of salt

SERVES 4 TO 6

These brownies are easy to make, yet taste incredible.
Rich and full of flavor, they're a firm favorite at home
—perfect for those days where nothing but chocolate
will do! As well as being extremely high in antioxidants,
cacao is also known to be a mood-booster.

Line a 11-by-8-in (27-by-20-cm) brownie pan with
parchment paper. Instead of a brownie pan, you could
use a loaf pan and make thicker brownie chunks.
   Blitz the nuts together in a food processor until they
form small crumbs. Add the dates and process until the
mixture starts to stick together.
   Add the remaining ingredients and process on high
speed until it turns a lovely, gooey chocolate brown. Press
into the lined pan and chill to firm up, at least 2 hours.
Turn out when chilled and slice into squares.

PARTY CUPCAKES WITH CACAO BUTTER ICING

⅓ cup (80 g) coconut oil, softened
Scant ½ cup (80 g) superfine sugar
2 large eggs, lightly beaten
1 tsp vanilla extract
Scant 1 cup (110 g) gluten-free flour
1 to 2 Tbsp almond milk

FOR THE BUTTER FROSTING
½ cup (65 g) cashews, soaked in
   cold water for 2 hours
3 Tbsp cacao butter, melted
2 tsp honey
½ tsp vanilla extract
2 tsp coconut oil
3 Tbsp warm water

MAKES 12 CUPCAKES

When you think of birthday parties, the first thing
that comes to mind is CAKE! Of course, growing
up and going to friends' parties, I couldn't eat the
cakes on offer and would turn up with my own little
package of homemade cupcakes and other goodies.

Preheat the oven 350°F (180°C). Line a 12-cup cupcake
tray with paper liners.
   Put the coconut oil and sugar in a mixing bowl and
beat using an electric whisk. Beat in the eggs, a little
at a time, then add the vanilla extract. Fold in the flour,
adding the milk if the batter is too thick, then spoon into
the cupcake liners. Bake in the oven for 10 to 15 minutes,
until golden and the tops spring back when lightly
pressed. Let cool completely.
   Place all the frosting ingredients except the water in a
blender and blitz until smooth. Slowly add the water until
it reaches a butter frosting consistency. Let stand in a
cool place, before piping over the cupcakes.
   Any leftover frosting can be stored in the refrigerator,
or frozen.

This may at first seem a little bit indulgent but it's the perfect treat after a tough week. Each ingredient is as natural and wholesome as possible—what could be better? Pears taste utterly delicious when paired with rich chocolate.

CHOCOLATE AND PEAR UPSIDE DOWN CAKE

½ cup (125 g) coconut oil, melted
¾ cup (150 g) superfine sugar
2 ripe pears, peeled, cored, and cut into eighths (well-drained canned are fine)
4 large eggs
2¼ cups (200 g) ground almonds
½ cup (50 g) slivered almonds
¼ cup (25 g) raw cacao powder
2 tsp gluten-free baking powder
1¾ oz (50 g) semisweet chocolate (at least 70% cocoa solids, melted, to decorate

SERVES 8

Preheat the oven to 350°F (180°C). Lightly grease a nonstick 9-in (23-cm) square cake pan.

Mix together ¼ cup (50 g) of the melted coconut oil with ¼ cup (50 g) of the sugar, then pour the mixture over the bottom of the cake pan. Arrange the pears slices neatly in rows to cover the bottom of the cake pan, then set aside.

Break the eggs into a bowl, add the remaining sugar, and beat using an electric whisk on high speed until light and creamy in consistency, 5 to 10 minutes.

Whisk in the remaining melted coconut oil, then carefully fold in the ground almonds, slivered almonds, cacao powder, and baking powder.

Pour the batter into the prepared pan over the pears, ensuring the top is level. Bake in the oven for 30 to 35 minutes, or until a skewer comes out clean. Let cool slightly in the cake pan before turning out onto a serving plate. Drizzle the melted dark chocolate over the pears and then serve with crème fraîche.

DOUBLE CHOCOLATE PEANUT BUTTER COOKIES

½ cup (100 g) coconut oil, melted
1⅛ cups (90 g) oat flour (or gluten-free oats processed for 1 to 2 minutes to make a flour)
Scant 1 cup (80 g) ground almonds
2 Tbsp raw cacao powder
½ tsp baking soda
4 Tbsp stevia
¼ cup (50 g) coconut sugar
2 eggs, beaten
½ cup (120 g) chocolate peanut butter (or regular peanut butter)
Scant 1 cup (100 g) cacao nibs or semisweet chocolate chunks

MAKES 8 TO 10 COOKIES

GF | WF | LF | VEG

There are often times when all I want is to eat cookies. These peanut butter ones are much healthier than any store-bought version and are a real treat on rainy Sunday afternoons. Just try and resist eating them all!

Preheat the oven to 350°F (180°C). Lightly grease two cookie sheets and line with parchment paper.

Put the oat flour, ground almonds, cacao powder, baking soda, stevia, and coconut sugar in a bowl and mix. In a separate bowl, mix together the egg, peanut butter, and coconut oil until smooth.

Fold the dry ingredients into the wet until just combined, then stir in the cacao nibs or chocolate chunks. Spoon a tablespoon of cookie dough for each cookie on the prepared cookie sheets, leaving room for them to spread. Bake in the oven for 8 to 10 minutes, or until cooked. Let cool, then enjoy.

OAT AND RAISIN COOKIE CHUNKS

⅓ cup (75 g) coconut oil
Heaping ⅛ cup (50 g) honey
¼ cup (50 g) coconut sugar
⅓ cup (40 g) all-purpose flour
Scant ½ cup (40 g) ground almonds
¾ tsp baking soda
Scant 2 cups (150 g) oats
½ tsp Himalayan salt
1 egg, lightly beaten
1 cup (175 g) raisins
2¾ oz (75 g) semisweet chocolate (at least 70% cocoa solids), broken into small pieces

MAKES ABOUT 30 CHUNKS

GF | WF | VEG

These delicious cookie chunks full of oat and raisin goodness are great for snacking on with friends. Quick, easy, and very moreish! The only challenge is in not eating the lot ... and before Jack and Tom get to them!

Preheat the oven to 350°F (180°C). Lightly grease a cookie sheet and line with parchment paper.

Melt the coconut oil in a small saucepan over low heat, then remove from the heat and mix in the honey and coconut sugar.

In a separate bowl, combine the flour, ground almonds, baking soda, oats, and salt. Stir in the melted coconut oil, honey, and sugar mixture, then add the egg and raisins and mix well. Stir in the chocolate and combine, using a wooden spoon.

Spread the dough onto the lined cookie sheet and level it out, to ensure even cooking. Bake for 12 minutes, then let cool completely before breaking into chunks.

CHOCOLATE GRANOLA SQUARES

FOR THE GRANOLA SQUARES
1¼ cups (100 g) gluten-free oats
¼ cup (60 g) coconut oil, melted
¼ cup (25 g) almonds, coarsely
　　chopped
¼ cup (25 g) mixed seeds of choice
　　(sunflower, chia, pumpkin, etc.)
1 tsp ground cinnamon
3 Tbsp runny honey or agave
　　nectar (optional)

FOR THE CHOCOLATE SAUCE
2 Tbsp coconut oil, melted
⅓ cup (30 g) raw cacao powder

MAKES ABOUT 30 SQUARES

These granola squares are the perfect sweet treat to reach for when you hit that midafternoon slump. You know, the kind that usually has you running for the cookie tin.

Lightly grease and line a 13½-by-8-in (34-by-20-cm) cookie sheet with parchment paper.

　　Mix all the ingredients for the granola squares together until well combined, then spread out on the lined cookie sheet, ensuring there are no gaps.

　　Mix the coconut oil and cacao together for the sauce, then drizzle on top of the granola.

　　Chill in the refrigerator for 2 hours to set (or in the freezer for 1 hour if you're feeling impatient) before cutting into squares. Store in the refrigerator or freezer, otherwise the granola squares will soften and melt.

RAISIN AND PECAN MUFFINS

1 cup (120 g) self-rising flour
½ tsp gluten-free baking powder
¼ cup (40 g) packed brown sugar
1 large egg, lightly beaten
¼ cup (50 g) coconut oil, melted
7 Tbsp (100 ml) almond milk
⅓ cup (40 g) pecans, in pieces
⅔ cup (120 g) golden raisins
Finely grated zest of 1 large orange

MAKES 10 MUFFINS

Although these little muffins are gluten- and dairy-free, they are so tasty that you'd never know it. The orange zest really livens things up, and I love the way they make my house smell as they bake.

Preheat the oven to 350°F (180°C). Line a muffin tray with 10 paper liners or lightly grease a silicon muffin tray.

　　Put the flour, baking powder, and sugar in a bowl and mix. In a separate bowl, mix together the egg, coconut oil, and almond milk until smooth. Fold the dry ingredients into the wet until just combined. Take care not to overwork the mixture or the muffins won't rise.

　　Fold in the pecans, golden raisins, and orange zest until just combined. Divide the batter between the prepared muffin liners. Bake in the oven for 15 minutes, until springy to the touch. Let cool, then devour.

I have quite a sweet tooth but I don't really want to indulge in processed, sugary ice pops and ice creams. Making these fruit ice pops are the perfect fix, particularly on long, hot summer days.

CACAO BANANA POPSICLES

2 Tbsp coconut oil, melted
1/3 cup (30 g) raw cacao powder
6 bananas

FOR THE TOPPINGS
Pistachios, goji berries, cacao nibs, raisins (anything you fancy!)

MAKES 12 POPSICLES

Place the melted coconut oil and cacao in a bowl and stir together until smooth and lump-free. Line a cookie sheet with parchment paper.

Peel the bananas, cut in half, and slide onto popsicle sticks or toothpicks. Dunk the bananas on sticks into the melted cacao mixture. Sprinkle over your favorite topping, place on the cookie sheet, and chill in the refrigerator to set, for about 1 hour.

Remove your popsicles from the refrigerator and enjoy!

LUCY'S PANTRY

BLITZED RAW DRESSING

This dressing really brings salads to life, especially arugula with brown rice or quinoa, although it is also great with my Brown Rice Pasta Bake (see page 113). Adding avocados to a salad dressing not only makes it wonderfully creamy, but also loads it with healthy fats, which are great for glowing skin.

MAKES 4 SERVINGS

1 ripe avocado
Juice of 2 lemons
1 cup (50 g) chopped cilantro
2 tsp Dijon mustard
2 tsp agave nectar or runny honey
3½ Tbsp (50 ml) water
Pinch each of Himalayan salt
    black pepper

Put all the ingredients, except the water, with salt and pepper to taste, into a blender, then blend together until smooth. Slowly pour in the water, with the motor running, until it reaches your desired consistency; you may need a little more water, depending on the size of the avocado.

This is best served immediately, but otherwise store the dressing in the refrigerator in a recycled Lucy Bee jar. Give the jar a good shake before serving.

LEMON GARLIC DRESSING

This dressing gets better with age, so store in a recycled Lucy Bee jar ready for the week ahead. If you are taking a salad into work for lunch, take the dressing in a separate container to stop your salad ending up soggy. You can add chopped fresh herbs such as parsley, chives, and cilantro to this dressing.

MAKES 10 SERVINGS

⅝ cup (150 ml) Udo's or olive oil
⅓ cup (80 ml) lemon juice
2 large garlic cloves, pureed
2 Tbsp agave nectar or honey
2 Tbsp Dijon mustard
Pinch each of Himalayan salt and
    black pepper

Put all the ingredients, with salt and pepper to taste, into a blender bottle (vitamin shaker) and shake thoroughly, then pour into an empty Lucy Bee jar and store in the refrigerator.

CHILI DIPPING SAUCE

This is a quick, healthy, and easy dipping sauce for shrimp or chicken, but it can also be used as a dressing for salads and vegetables. This sauce can be stored in a recycled Lucy Bee jar in the refrigerator ready for the week ahead. If you prefer less spice in your sauce, just leave out the green chile.

MAKES 4 SERVINGS

1 tsp finely chopped ginger
1 garlic clove, crushed
1 green chile, seeded
    and minced
6 Tbsp (90 ml) tamari sauce
Juice of ½ lemon
2 tsp agave nectar or runny honey
2 tsp sesame oil
Pinch of ground black pepper

Put all the ingredients into a blender bottle (vitamin shaker) and shake thoroughly, then pour into a recycled Lucy Bee jar and store in the refrigerator.

INDIAN-STYLE COCONUT OIL

Indian spices are wonderful for adding flavor to dishes; they're also great for a health boost too.

MAKES 4 SERVINGS

4 Tbsp (60ml) coconut oil
1 oz (30 g) ginger, skin scraped, chopped
2 garlic cloves, peeled
2 red chiles, seeded, or 1 tsp chili powder
1 tsp cumin seeds
1 tsp ground coriander
5 cardamom pods
1 tsp ground turmeric
2 shallots, chopped
Pinch of Himalayan salt and black pepper

Blitz all the ingredients to a smooth paste in a food processor. Place in a recycled Lucy Bee jar and refrigerate.

SPANISH-STYLE COCONUT OIL

This oil gives food a deep, smoky flavor. Stir into soups or casseroles or use it as a sauce with your favorite meals.

MAKES 4 SERVINGS

4 Tbsp (60 ml) coconut oil
Pinch of saffron threads
1 garlic clove, peeled
1 Tbsp smoked paprika
2¾ oz (75 g) roasted red bell peppers, peeled
1 tsp ground fennel
Pinch of salt and black pepper

Blitz everything to a smooth paste in a food processor. Place in a recycled Lucy Bee jar and refrigerate.

ANCHOVY AND ROSEMARY COCONUT OIL

This is a wonderful marinade for meats, particularly lamb. The saltiness from the anchovies really brings out the rich flavors and makes for an all-round lip-smacking dinner. Add a teaspoon to soups, to liven them up, or use to fry chicken or fish.

MAKES 4 SERVINGS

4 Tbsp (60ml) coconut oil, softened
1 x 1¾-oz (50-g) can anchovies in oil, drained
2 garlic cloves, peeled
¾ oz (20 g) rosemary, leaves only
2 shallots, chopped
Finely grated zest and juice of ½ lemon
Pinch each of Himalayan salt and black pepper

Blitz all the ingredients to a smooth paste in a food processor. Place in a recycled Lucy Bee jar and refrigerate.

RASPBERRY CHIPOTLE SAUCE

This can be used as both a sweet and savory sauce, although most people never think to use it in desserts. Chipotle peppers, which are smoke-dried jalapeño chiles, add a real depth of flavor and heat that I love (I sometimes add double the amount, or the whole can here!).

MAKES 12 SERVINGS

1 Tbsp coconut oil
1 large onion, grated
2 large garlic cloves, minced
5¼ oz (150 g) chipotle peppers in adobo, chopped
4 cups (500 g) raspberries
7 Tbsp (100 ml) cider vinegar
⅔ cup (150 g) coconut sugar (or the darkest sugar you have)
Himalayan salt and black pepper

Melt the coconut oil in a heavy-bottom pan over medium heat. Add the onion and cook until soft and starting to brown. Stir in the garlic and cook for a couple of minutes.

Add the chipotle peppers, stir, then add the raspberries. Cook for a few minutes until bubbling. Add the vinegar and sugar, then slowly bring to a boil. Reduce the heat and cook until reduced and thickened, about 20 minutes. Remove from the heat and let cool.

For a seed-free, smooth sauce (although I leave it as it is), push the mixture through a fine strainer using the back of a spoon. When cool, transfer to a recycled Lucy Bee jar and store in the refrigerator.

THAI-STYLE COCONUT OIL

This is simply a flavor and aroma sensation! I stir this oil into soups or fry my favorite meats in it. It tastes great served on the side of your favorite meals for an extra boost! As it keeps really well, scale up the ingredients to make more.

MAKES 4 SERVINGS

2 red chiles, seeded,
   or 1 tsp chili powder
2 garlic cloves, peeled
1 lemongrass stalk, coarse outer
   leaves removed, minced
1 oz (30 g) ginger, skin scraped,
   chopped
2 shallots, chopped
3 kaffir lime leaves, crumbled
Juice of 1 lime
½ bunch of fresh cilantro,
   including the stalks
4 Tbsp (60 ml) coconut oil,
   softened

Blitz all the ingredients together in a food processor to a smooth paste. Store in a recycled Lucy Bee jar in the refrigerator.

SPICY COCONUT OIL HARISSA

Harissa is a deliciously spicy and peppery paste—sometimes extremely hot, but this version can be as fiery as you wish. You can also experiment with other spices, such as coriander. I use this as the basis for many quick and healthy suppers—it adds a real depth of flavor to chicken or fish. Try stirring a spoonful into soups for a completely different flavor sensation. It keeps well stored refrigerated.

MAKES 4 SERVINGS

2 red chiles, seeded,
   or 1 tsp chili powder
4 garlic cloves, peeled
3½ oz (100 g) red roasted bell
   peppers, from a jar (leave the
   chargrilled bits on)
1 tsp cumin seeds
1 tsp caraway seeds
1 Tbsp tomato paste
2 tsp smoked paprika
4 Tbsp (60 ml) coconut oil,
   softened

Blitz all the ingredients together in a food processor to a smooth paste. Store in a recycled Lucy Bee jar in the refrigerator.

GF WF DF LF V

COCONUT OIL SALSA VERDE

Salsa verde is a delicious, punchy sauce made with herbs that tastes divine with meats or fish, especially on the barbecue. However, anything goes, and I also like to serve this with roasted vegetables, roasted chicken, and broiled halloumi. It can be a great way of using up any green herbs you have left lurking in the back of the refrigerator.

MAKES 4 SERVINGS

1 cup (30 g) parsley leaves
1 cup (30 g) cilantro leaves
1 tsp capers
1 shallot, chopped
1 cup (10 g) dill
3 anchovy fillets in oil
Juice of ½ lemon
4 Tbsp (60 ml) coconut oil
Himalayan salt and ground
   black pepper

Put all the ingredients in a food processor, with salt and pepper to taste, and blitz to a smooth paste. Store in a recycled Lucy Bee jar.

WHITE SAUCE

My style of cooking is quick and easy, so for this white sauce all the ingredients are added at once. This way, you never get those lumps that can happen when making a roux.

MAKES 2 CUPS (500 ML)
Scant ¼ cup (40 g) coconut oil
⅓ cup (40 g) gluten-free
    all-purpose flour
2 cups (500 ml) milk

Place all the ingredients in a large saucepan. Over medium heat, using a balloon whisk and whisking continously, combine the oil, flour, and milk to a sauce—after 8 minutes the sauce will start to thicken. Continue cooking and stirring for another 2 minutes.

SUN-DRIED TOMATO PESTO

My family and I are huge fans of pesto; it just goes so well with all kinds of foods, including my Goat Cheese and Arugula Frittata (see page 62). Think outside the pasta box and use it with cauliflower pizza, zucchini, stirred into soups, or spread on toast, as well as on pasta. It's a great food to have handy in the refrigerator.

MAKES 4 SERVINGS
Scant 1 cup (100 g) pine nuts
3 oz (80 g) Parmesan or any hard
    lactose-free cheese, chopped
¼ cup (50 g) coconut oil, melted
4½ oz (125 g) sun-dried tomatoes
Scant ⅔ cup (25 g) basil leaves
1 garlic clove, finely sliced
Juice of 1 lemon

Place the pine nuts in a dry frying pan over medium heat and toast until golden, then tip onto a plate.
    Put the Parmesan in a food processor and blitz, then add the pine nuts and remaining ingredients, except the lemon juice, and blitz once more, until combined but still with a little texture. Pour in the lemon juice and blitz for a final 30 seconds,. Scrape into an airtight container, such as a recycled Lucy Bee jar, and store in the refrigerator for up to 1 week.

SUN-DRIED TOMATO HUMMUS

I adore hummus and eat it with so many things, from bread and olives to chicken, carrots, salads—the list is endless … This hummus keeps for a week in the refrigerator, but remove it to room temperature an hour before eating, or the coconut oil will cause it to go hard. Stir it well before serving, maybe adding a little more lemon juice.

MAKES 4 SERVINGS
14-oz (400-g) can chickpeas,
    drained and rinsed
4 tsp coconut oil
¼ cup (60 g) tahini
1 garlic clove, minced
1¾ oz (50 g) sun-dried tomatoes
3½ Tbsp (50 ml) lemon juice
Himalayan salt and black pepper

Place all the ingredients in a food processor, with salt and pepper to taste, and blend until smooth. Serve, topped with a drizzle of olive oil, some toasted pine nuts, and a shake of paprika, if desired.

BOLOGNESE SAUCE

This dish is one of my ultimate comfort foods. I love using it for a huge variety of dishes, not just with spaghetti. It's great in a shepherd's pie or lasagna and my Brown Rice Pasta Bake (see page 113). It freezes well.

SERVES 4 TO 6
2 Tbsp coconut oil
7 oz (200 g) onions, chopped
2 garlic cloves, chopped
3½ oz (100 g) celery, diced
7 oz (200 g) carrots, chopped
1 lb 2 oz (500 g) ground beef
1 Tbsp dried mixed herbs
7 Tbsp (100 ml) red wine (optional)
5¼ oz (150 g) sun-dried tomatoes, finely chopped
14-oz (400-g) can chopped tomatoes
Himalayan salt and black pepper

Preheat the oven to 275°F (140°C).

Heat the coconut oil in a heavy-bottom saucepan, then add the onions, garlic, celery, and carrots and sauté for 10 minutes over low heat, stirring occasionally, until softened and lightly colored.

Tip in the meat and cook until browned, then stir in the mixed herbs and season well with the salt and pepper. Pour in the red wine, if using, then increase the heat and cook, uncovered, until all the liquid has evaporated.

Add the sun-dried tomatoes and canned tomatoes, then bring to a boil, cover, and cook in the oven for 2 hours, until all the flavors have mingled. Alternatively, cook on the stove over low heat.

QUICK-COOK TOMATO SAUCE

This is the perfect sauce to whip up in the evening and serve with whatever takes your fancy; it's ideal for pasta, pizzas, or meatballs. Add one or more of your favorite herbs; tarragon is good if serving with chicken, or sage if serving with sausages.

SERVES 4 TO 6
2 Tbsp coconut oil
6 large garlic cloves, crushed
2 x 14-oz (400-g) cans chopped tomatoes
Juice of ½ lemon
1 tsp mixed dried herbs or 3 fresh thyme sprigs (optional)
Himalayan salt and black pepper

Melt the coconut oil in a heavy-bottom pan over medium heat, then add the garlic and sauté until soft but not colored.

Add the chopped tomatoes and lemon juice, then stir together. Season with salt and lots of black pepper, then stir through the herbs, if using.

Bring to a boil, then cover and simmer over low heat for 20 minutes.

VARIATIONS

Spice it up by adding dried red pepper flakes, cayenne pepper, or fresh chile peppers. Or stir through anchovies, chorizo, or pancetta (add after the garlic, and sauté well before adding the tomatoes) or olives.

SLOW-COOK TOMATO SAUCE

If you have time to let this sauce simmer for an hour or so, it's really worth waiting for. The wine adds a twist to a classic tomato sauce, with the paprika giving it a delicious kick. I first made this with leftover wine—better for me than drinking it!

SERVES 4 TO 6
2 Tbsp coconut oil
1 large onion, minced
2 large garlic cloves, minced
2 x 14-oz (400-g) cans chopped tomatoes
1 level tsp hot smoked paprika
⅝ cup (150 ml) red wine
2 tsp soft brown sugar
3 fresh thyme sprigs
Himalayan salt and black pepper

Melt the coconut oil in a heavy-bottom pan over medium heat. Add the onion and sauté until softened but not browning much.

Add the garlic and cook for a few more minutes, stirring every so often so that it doesn't catch. Tip in the chopped tomatoes, paprika, wine, and sugar and stir to combine. Season with salt and pepper, then add the thyme. Cover and simmer over very low heat for 1 hour, or until reduced and thickened.

HOMEMADE CHICKEN BROTH

I like to make up huge batches of this perfect base for soups, sauces, and gravies, to freeze in individual portions. Chicken soup is an ideal use for this broth, and is one of the most comforting, nourishing foods imaginable. It reminds me of days snuggled on the couch when I was ill, with my mom bringing me bowls of soup.

MAKES 4½ CUPS (1 LITER)
2¼ lb (1 kg) chicken bones and/or carcasses
2 onions, minced
4 carrots, minced
2 celery stalks, minced
2 garlic cloves, minced
About 12 black peppercorns
2 or 3 cloves
2 dried or fresh bay leaves
A few fresh or dried thyme sprigs
A few parsley stalks

Put the chicken bones in a large saucepan, add all the chopped vegetables, and cover with cold water. Bring to a boil, skimming off any scum that appears on the surface, using a spoon.
  Add the peppercorns, cloves, bay, thyme, and parsley. Cover, turn down to low simmer, and cook for a couple of hours (or longer, if you wish). Strain the stock through a strainer into another saucepan or container.
  Let cool a little, then remove the fat by laying paper towels on the surface. If desired, reduce the broth over high heat to make it stronger. Portion into the required amounts and freeze when cool.

HOMEMADE CURRY POWDER

You can make your blend as hot or mild as you like; just add more chili.

MAKES 2 TO 3 TBSP
1 tsp cumin seeds
1 tsp coriander seeds
1 tsp mustard seeds
1 tsp fenugreek seeds
1 tsp cardamom pods
1 tsp ground ginger
1 tsp ground turmeric
½ to 1 tsp chili powder, depending on how much heat you want

Put a heavy-bottom frying pan over medium heat and add all the seeds, moving them around so that they don't burn. After about 1 minute, you will get a wonderful, fragrant aroma. Remove from the heat and let cool.
  Blitz the cooled seeds to a fine powder in a spice or coffee grinder. Mix in the remaining spices and give a final blitz. Store in a recycled Lucy Bee jar.

GARAM MASALA

For a flavor boost, add garam masala at the end of a recipe.

MAKES 2 TO 3 TBSP
1 Tbsp green cardamom pods
2-in (5-cm) stick cinnamon
1 tsp cumin seeds
1 tsp black peppercorns
½ tsp grated nutmeg
½ tsp whole cloves

Blitz all the spices to a fine powder in a spice or coffee grinder. Store in a recycled Lucy Bee jar.

BAHARAT SPICE MIX

This is a popular spice blend used throughout the Middle East. Baharat is the Arabic word for spices.

MAKES 2 TO 3 TBSP
2 tsp ground black pepper
2 tsp paprika
½ tsp ground cumin
½ tsp coriander seeds
½ tsp cloves
Seeds of 3 cardamom pods

Place all the ingredients in a mortar and pestle and grind until crushed, but not too fine.

DUKKAH SPICED SEED MIX

The word dukkah means to crush or to pound in Egyptian, so is an apt name for this mix of toasted nuts and spices.

MAKES 2 TO 3 TBSP
¼ cup (25 g) hazelnuts
1 tsp cumin seeds
1 tsp coriander seeds
2 Tbsp sesame seeds
½ tsp Himalayan salt

Toast the hazelnuts and cumin and coriander seeds in a dry pan for 3 minutes. Place all the ingredients in a mortar and pestle and grind until crushed, but not too fine.

MANGO SALSA

This refreshing salsa livens up burgers, broiled meats, marinated chicken or fish. It's a great dip for sweet potato nachos.

SERVES 2 TO 4

1 red onion, minced
Juice of 1 lime
7 oz (200 g) mango flesh
1 green chile, seeded and
    minced (optional)
1 ripe avocado
Bunch of cilantro, leaves chopped

Mix the onion and lime juice in a bowl and let marinate for 4 hours (this softens and sweetens the onions). Chop the mango and avocado into small pieces. Add with the remaining ingredients and season. Serve immediately.

ALMOND MILK

As store-bought milks often don't contain many actual almonds, it pays to make your own.

MAKES 4½ CUPS (1 LITER)

Scant 2 cups (200 g) almonds
    (soaked for 12 hours in just
    enough water to cover)
4½ cups (1 liter) water
1 tsp runny honey or agave
    nectar (optional)

Drain the almonds. Transfer with the 4½ cups (1 liter) water to a high-speed blender and blend until smooth. Strain the almond liquid through a fine strainer, cheesecloth, leaving behind the almond meal. Stir through the honey, if using. Pour the milk into a glass bottle and chill for 2 days.

HEALTHY SEED MIX

We now know that good fats are essential for a healthy diet, and this moreish mix is a great way to get a balanced combination of Omega-3, -6, and -9 into your diet, as well as loads of trace nutrients and fiber. I use it to enrich my baking, add to my oatmeal or pancakes, or to sprinkle into my crumble toppings. It's also great on top of smoothies or yogurt and, because it's been blitzed together, is easier to digest.

MAKES 1 JAR

1½ cups (250 g) flaxseeds
Scant ½ cup (60 g) sesame seeds
½ cup (60 g) sunflower seeds
½ cup (60 g) hemp seeds
½ cup (60 g) pumpkin seeds

Blitz all the ingredients to a powder in a nut and seed grinder (or coffee grinder). Store in the refrigerator (to retain goodness) in a recycled Lucy Bee jar.

SALTED CHOCOLATE ALMOND BUTTER

This delicious almond butter is rich, chocolaty, and incredibly tasty. It's very good for dunking strawberries or apples, but I love it so much I've even been known to sit with a jar and a spoon. You have been warned ...

SERVES 4

Scant 3¼ cups (350 g) roasted
    almonds
1 Tbsp coconut oil
2¼ oz (60 g) semisweet chocolate
    (70% cocoa solids), chopped
2 Tbsp raw cacao powder
2 to 3 tsp honey or maple syrup
½ tsp vanilla extract
1 tsp Himalayan salt

Place the almonds in a high-powered blender and blitz to your desired consistency, scraping down the sides as you go. I like it fairly liquid, but you can have it crunchy and chunky if you prefer.
    Gently melt the coconut oil and chocolate together until smooth. Add to the blender with the remaining ingredients, then blitz until combined. Taste and add more salt or honey, if needed. Pour the almond butter into an airtight container and chill for up to 1 week—if it lasts that long!

CHOCOLATE AND PEAR JAM

This is incredibly indulgent and feels a little decadent when spread over gluten-free toast at breakfast. This delicious jam is one of my favorite chocolaty treats.

MAKES 1 JAR

3 pears, peeled, cored, and diced
½ to ¾ cup (100 to 150 g) stevia, to taste
Juice ½ lemon
Juice ½ orange
Pinch of ground cinnamon
½ tsp Himalayan salt
1 Tbsp coconut oil
5¼ oz (150 g) semisweet chocolate (70% cocoa solids), chopped

Put the diced pears into a large saucepan, then stir in the stevia, lemon, and orange juice and cinnamon. Place over medium heat until it starts to simmer, then remove and pour into a bowl.

Stir in the salt, coconut oil, and chocolate, and mix until the chocolate has melted. Cover and let cool, then place in the refrigerator overnight, for the mixture to thicken.

Pour the mixture back into a saucepan, bring to a boil, and bubble for about 40 minutes, until it reaches 32°F (105°C) on a sugar thermometer, or is a spreadable, jamlike consistency, stirring frequently so that it doesn't catch and burn. Let cool briefly before pouring into a jar. Cool, then cover and chill for up to 1 week.

FLAXSEED BREAD WITH ANCHOVY AND ROSEMARY

Being celiac, I've never been able to indulge in those freshly baked loaves from the bakers, but here is a gluten-free loaf to enjoy. The flavors work really well together, and nothing quite beats the smell of homemade bread baking in the oven ...

SERVES 4 TO 6

1⅓ cups (225 g) milled flaxseed
1 Tbsp baking powder
5 large eggs
5 Tbsp (75 ml) water
⅓ cup (70 g) coconut oil, melted
6 anchovy fillets in oil, chopped
2 Tbsp dried or chopped fresh rosemary

Preheat the oven to 350°F (180°C). Line a baking sheet with parchment paper.

Combine the flaxseed and baking powder in a mixing bowl.

In a separate bowl, beat the eggs, water, coconut oil, anchovy fillets, and rosemary together, setting aside a little rosemary for the top of the loaf.

Stir the wet ingredients into the dry mixture to combine, then let stand for about 3 minutes to thicken up. Remove the dough from the bowl and shape into a rounded, loaflike shape. Place on the lined sheet, sprinkle over the reserved rosemary, and bake for 25 minutes, until a knife inserted into the center comes out clean.

GLUTEN-FREE FLATBREADS

Chickpea flour, also known as garbanzo bean flour, gram flour, or besan, is made from ground chickpeas. Used in many countries, it's a staple ingredient in Indian and Pakistani cuisines. These simple flatbreads are naturally gluten-free, inexpensive to make, and a great alternative to use with dips or curries.

SERVES 10

1 cup (150 g) chickpea flour, plus extra for dusting
⅔ cup (100 g) rice flour
¼ tsp cayenne pepper
1 Tbsp minced cilantro
1 tsp Himalayan salt
7 Tbsp (100 ml) water
2 Tbsp coconut oil

Mix the chickpea flour, rice flour, cayenne, cilantro, and salt in a large bowl. Slowly pour in the water, stirring all the time until smooth. You need a nice dough that you can roll, not too sticky or too dry, so you may or may not need to add a splash more water.

Roll into a sausage shape, cut into 10 equal pieces, and shape into walnut-size balls.

Dust a counter with chickpea flour and, using a rolling pin, roll each ball into a round, thin pancake. Keep turning and dusting them so that they don't stick.

Heat a non-stick frying pan over medium heat and add a small amount of the coconut oil until melted. Add as many flatbreads as will comfortably fit in the pan (2 or 3) and fry for a couple of minutes on each side, until they slightly bubble and start to brown.

Add some more coconut oil and cook the remaining flatbreads.

NUTRITIONAL INFORMATION

ALMONDS are high in heart-healthy monounsaturated fats. **Almond flour** is a good gluten-free baking ingredient and keeps cakes deliciously moist. **Almond milk** is my favorite dairy-free option to add to breakfasts and smoothies or shakes. It also happens to be a good source of protein and is rich in riboflavin, a form of vitamin B that is proven to work with other nutrients to regulate muscle strength and growth. Almond milk may even give you glowing skin and hair, thanks to its vitamin E content.

ANCHOVIES pack in a lot of flavor for such a small fish, so you only need to use a small amount. They are rich in omega-3s, which can prevent inflammation, and also in magnesium and calcium, for strong bones and teeth.

ARUGULA is packed with vital phytochemicals, vitamins, and minerals. It's also a wonderful source of folates and vitamin C, helping to protect from disease.

ASPARAGUS is a great way to get in your dosage of folate, vitamins A, C, E, and K, and chromium.

AVOCADO is one of the most nutritious foods you'll ever come across. Rich in healthy fats to reduce inflammation, it's high in fiber and vitamins such as K, C, and E, and is also loaded with potassium. It can even help you to absorb nutrients from other plant-based foods.

BAKING SODA isn't just a great home remedy for teeth whitening, insect bites, and as a natural deodorant, it also neutralizes stomach acid to treat heartburn and indigestion

BANANAS are great for your body and can aid digestion, as well as giving you a real bounce in energy. The potassium can protect against muscle cramps.

BASIL has antibacterial as well as anti-inflammatory properties, which are great for reducing swelling, and is known to have antiaging properties. It is also a good way to get your vitamin A, which can protect from free radicals.

BEET lends the most beautiful color to dishes and is also incredibly good for you. It contains a unique group of antioxidants known as betacyanins (which happen to give it the vibrant color), and it also supports the liver, purifies the blood, and improves circulation.

BLACKBERRIES have one of the highest antioxidant levels of all fruits, while they are also rich in minerals and vitamins that give a youthful glow. Blackberries are even high in vitamin K, meaning they can help to aid muscle relaxation.

BLUEBERRIES are known as a superfood and certainly pack an incredibly powerful nutritious punch. They are extremely high in antioxidants, which work to fight free radicals, and loaded with vitamin C to boost collagen formation and keep your immune system happy.

BOK CHOY, also known as pak choi, is a leafy Chinese cabbage popular in health circles because of its phytonutrients, vitamins, and health-boosting antioxidants. It's also rich in potassium and iron.

BROCCOLI is incredibly good for you. It has a blend of phytonutrients and is high in mood-boosting vitamin D. It also contains a certain flavonoid which can lessen the impact of allergies and reactions on the body. And one serving can give you 150% of your daily needs of vitamin C.

BROWN RICE is far healthier than white rice, which has been stripped of all goodness and nutrients during the refining process. Brown rice is also high in selenium, which cuts the risk of developing diseases such as heart disease, as well as manganese, which helps the body to process fats. The fiber content also helps to keep you feeling fuller for longer.

BROWN RICE PASTA, my favorite gluten-free pasta, tastes every bit as delicious as the less healthy white kind. Made from just brown rice and water, it contains the same nutrients and health benefits of rice and so is an excellent source of manganese for energy production, selenium for immune function, and magnesium, which helps to ease muscle aches and sleep problems such as insomnia.

BRUSSELS SPROUTS are a great way to get in some vitamins C and K: just one serving will give you your recommended daily allowance.

CACAO doesn't just taste delicious, it's extremely high in antioxidants, and flavanols and other components found in cacao can lower blood pressure and boost circulation. It's also a known mood-booster while the ancient Aztecs would even use it as an aphrodisiac.

CANNELLINI BEANS are good for bulking up dishes. They have an incredibly low GI, which means they keep you feeling full for hours, giving you energy long after you've eaten. The beans are also thought to have a detoxifying effect on the body, while being supercharged with antioxidants.

CAPERS are rich in the antioxidant quercetin, which has antibacterial and anti-inflammatory properties. They also give you a healthy dose of vitamins A and K.

CARAWAY SEEDS have long been used in traditional and ancient medicines because they're packed with vitamins, minerals, and goodness. They also contain essential oils, which are known to be antioxidant and also aid digestion.

CARDAMOM is deliciously fragrant and was used for centuries in Ayurvedic medicine as a treatment for mouth ulcers and digestive problems, among other things. It's also great for detoxifying the body as it helps to eliminate waste, and can even freshen the breath too!

CASHEWS and **CASHEW NUT BUTTER** are high in essential amino acids, heart-friendly monounsaturated fats, and minerals, particularly manganese, potassium, copper, iron, magnesium, zinc, and selenium.

CAULIFLOWER is full of healthy nutrients and vitamins, including vitamins C, K, and B6, and is anti-inflammatory, which helps the body to stay healthy. It is also a great source of omega-3 fatty acids and dietary fiber, and has been found to protect the lining of your stomach.

CELERIAC (celery root) is full of fiber to keep your insides happy, and is also high in vitamin K to boost the bones, as well as phosphorus, iron, calcium, and copper.

CHIA SEEDS contain so many nutrients for such tiny little things! They are high in fiber, calcium, and heart-healthy omega-3s, and also rich in quality protein—perfect for vegetarian or vegan diets. They are also loaded with antioxidants.

CHICKPEAS, so versatile and high in nutritional value, are one of the cheapest ingredients you can buy. They are high in both fiber and protein, and have a low GI, so work as a slow-release energy source.

CHIVES are nutrient-dense and contain choline, which can help to aid sleep and relax the muscles.

CIDER VINEGAR is an ancient remedy for all sorts of ailments. It's high in acetic acid, which is antimicrobial and can kill certain bacteria.

CINNAMON is known to be a good anti-inflammatory, which can be used to fight off infections or diseases and repair tissue damage. It packs a hefty antioxidant punch, while its natural antimicrobial properties can ward off candida and fight certain strains of E Coli. As a natural sweetener, it can also stabilize blood sugar levels.

CILANTRO/CORIANDER can be used to treat inflamed skin, lower bad cholesterol, and blood pressure, and also to strengthen the bones, owing to its calcium content.

COCONUT MILK is perfect for anyone with a dairy allergy. It's also high in a medium-chain saturated fatty acid (MCFA) called lauric acid, which is both antiviral and antibacterial. It is quickly turned into energy by the liver, meaning that it is less likely to be stored as fat by the body.

COCONUT SUGAR, from the coconut palm, is one of the most delicious natural sweeteners on the planet, adding an almost caramel-like taste to foods. Although it's relatively high in carbs and calories, it has a lower GI than some other sugars and tends to have less of an impact on your blood sugar levels. It's also far lower in fructose—a type of sugar which your body converts to fat quickly—than other sweeteners such as agave, and contains nutrients removed in refined sugar, such as iron, zinc, calcium, and potassium. **Dried shredded coconut** is a great way to sweeten dishes in a healthier way and I'll even use it in cakes and bakes to add flavor. It's also rich in iron and fiber.

COD is a great way of getting lean protein into your diet. It's a good source of my favorite omega-3s, known to keep your heart healthy, as well as of selenium and vitamin B12.

COFFEE is wonderful for giving you a much-needed dose of energy, as we all know, particularly first thing in the morning or before a mammoth workout.

CORNMEAL was once known as "the food of the poor," but this gluten-free Italian stallion is now used in all manner of dishes. Made from ground corn, it is a deep yellow color and is tasty, filling, and incredibly versatile.

CORNSTARCH is a good alternative in gluten-free cooking. It's high in fiber and iron, and also contains phosphorus, which supports healthy enzyme function.

CUMIN, like cardamom, can be used to help with digestion, as it activates the salivary glands. It's even thought to be a natural remedy for insomnia because its vitamin complex can help to relax and induce sleep.

DATES are not only nature's candies, they can help to relieve digestive problems such as constipation, while the minerals found in dates can help to boost bone and tooth strength. The iron content is also great for those who suffer from anemia.

DRIED RED PEPPER FLAKES are great for adding a kick to any dish, they are also known to boost the metabolism and control appetite. They can even reduce pain, thanks to their levels of capsaicin, which can reduce pain-signaling neurotransmitters in the brain to work like a painkiller.

EGGPLANTS are packed with vitamins, minerals, and fiber, as well as being rich in antioxidants, such as nasunin, which gives eggplant its purple color and can protect the fats in brain cell membranes.

EGGS are an inexpensive source of high-quality protein. Both the white and yolk are rich in vitamins and minerals, and the yolk is full of Omega-3 fatty acids. They are an excellent source of phosphorus, selenium, vitamins A, B2, B5, and B12, as well as choline, an important nutrient for brain function.

FENUGREEK has long been used as a medicinal remedy in parts of Asia. It contains muscle-building protein, vitamin C, potassium, and diosgenin.

FETA is made with sheep or goat milk and has a strong, salty taste, which means less is more. It's a great way to get calcium into your diet, and it's also rich in vitamin B12, for red blood cell production.

FIVE-SPICE contains fennel, which can regulate digestion and is also high in folate, cinnamon to balance out blood sugars, star anise to ramp up the immune system, and antiseptic cloves and peppercorns to neutralize free radicals.

FLAXSEED is high in heart-healthy Omega-3s, and also contains both soluble and insoluble fiber.

GARLIC isn't just for scaring vampires! In fact, it's full of body-loving benefits and is great for fighting off colds and flu too. It can also help to improve iron metabolism, and may help to lower blood pressure, or hypertension.

GINGER is the perfect home remedy for treating nausea and sickness—particularly good for moms-to-be—but can also help to ease symptoms of colic. Its anti-inflammatory properties also make it ideal for helping with joint or muscle pain, as well as coughs and colds.

GOLDEN RAISINS come from red grapes, so are high in antioxidants such as resveratrol, which has been found to be anti-inflammatory, as well as fighting against certain cancers and lowering bad cholesterol.

GRASS-FED BUTTER, which is becoming hugely popular, is rich in the little-known vitamin K2. I'm a true believer in eating **GRASS-FED MEAT** whenever possible. It's packed with health benefits and tends to be lower in fat than regular meat. It's also higher in conjugated linoleic acid (CLA), and heart-healthy Omega-3s.

HALLOUMI is high in calcium and is also a good source of protein for vegetarians.

HAZELNUTS are naturally sweet and tasty but are also incredibly nutritious, too. They're extremely high in energy (great for a pre- or postworkout snack) and monounsaturated fatty acids and essential fatty acid. As a great source of vitamin E, they're also perfect for making the skin glow.

HEMP SEEDS are wonderful for an energy boost—a perfect pre- or postworkout addition—and also high in protein.

KELP NOODLES are made from a seaweed that grows in deep waters and is popular in Asian dishes. They are high in dietary fiber, meaning they'll keep your digestive system happy and your tummy full.

KIWI are a fantastic beautifier as they're high in vitamin C, to boost collagen, and smooth out pesky wrinkles or lines. They can also help to relieve constipation and are even thought to help combat sleep problems.

LAMB, particularly grass-fed lamb, is surprisingly high in Omega-3s and also Omega-6 fatty acid conjugated linoleic acid (CLA), which can boost the immune system.

LEMONS are a natural immune booster and great for easing the symptoms of coughs, colds, and sore throats. They increase the body's iron absorption and can give you glowing, healthy skin.

LEMONGRASS has almost never-ending health benefits; it's packed with so much goodness that it can fight plenty of chronic conditions. It's both anti-inflammatory and antiseptic and is also fantastic at detoxifying the liver. It works wonders during the cold and flu season, as it's full of antimicrobial, antioxidant properties.

LENTILS are not only a cheap addition to bulk up meals, they're also high in nutrients, and a great way for vegetarians or vegans to get their protein. They give plenty of slow-release energy, and are low in fat and calories. They can also be used to lower cholesterol, improve digestion, and increase energy levels.

LIME is a citrus juice, full of vitamin C, is great at fighting off diseases and cold viruses, and can even help to give fresh, glowing skin. Lime also aids digestion and can relieve constipation.

LIVER contains very high quantities of retinol, a form of vitamin A, which can build up in the body and harm unborn babies, so should be avoided by pregnant women. For those who can safely consume liver, it's one of the most nutrient-dense foods imaginable. Not only is it a brilliant source of iron, it's also high in vitamin B12, which your body needs to create red blood cells and protein-building amino acids.

LUCUMA, a caramel-like sweetener that tastes similar to maple syrup, makes an amazing alternative to processed sugars. It has a low GI and many other health benefits too, including being high in antioxidants, fiber, and anti-inflammatories.

MANGO is wonderful at helping to clear up the skin and is also high in vitamin A, which is great for eye health. It can also normalize blood sugar levels and improve digestion, thanks to a series of enzymes that can break down proteins.

MANUKA HONEY, from New Zealand, is by far the most superior of the many honeys on the market. It has antibacterial and healing properties and works wonders on fighting bugs and other nasties. It's also high in antioxidants to protect us against free radicals.

MAPLE SYRUP is a perfect option for anyone with a sweet tooth. It's high in nutrients, including magnesium, potassium, zinc, and calcium.

MINT is brilliant for indigestion as it can soothe the stomach and also encourages the salivary glands to secrete digestive enzymes. It's also great for treating congestion—perfect

for when you're bunged up and full of cold.

MOZZARELLA is a great source of protein, fantastic for energy levels, and building muscle, but is also rich in bone-strengthening calcium and skin- and vision-loving niacin, riboflavin, thiamine, biotin, and vitamin B6.

MUSTARD is full of health benefits, and known to ease muscle aches and pains, as well as symptoms of psoriasis and respiratory problems. The seeds are high in Omega-3s and contain phytonutrients, while the selenium and magnesium found in them have anti-inflammatory effects.

NIGELLA seeds, also called black cumin, have for centuries been one of the most widely used medicinal seeds. The ancient Greek physician Dioscorides used them to treat headaches and toothaches. They're also commonly used to aid digestion, and they can even be used as a treatment for psoriasis and eczema.

NORI is a type of seaweed that is rich in protein (some of which comes from one of my favorite superfoods, spirulina) as well as high in iron and iodine.

OATS are not only cheap to buy but they're also the perfect breakfast food as they're fantastic at fueling the body and keeping you feeling full. Oats contain a special kind of fiber, which can lower cholesterol levels and stabilize blood sugar levels, meaning they can prevent huge spikes in blood sugar levels. They are also a great source of magnesium.

PAPRIKA offers a whole host of health benefits. It's high in beta-carotene, which the body converts into the skin-loving and wrinkle-zapping vitamin A. It can even be used in homemade face masks, to reduce fine lines and leave skin glowing!

PARSLEY is rich in many vital vitamins, including C, B12, K, and A, meaning that it is wonderful for keeping the immune system strong and strengthening your bones and nervous system.

PASSION FRUITS are a great way to get your vitamin C, which helps the body to fight flulike viruses and harmful free radicals. They're also a good source of vitamin A, which is good for the eyes.

PEARS are incredibly high in fiber, which can ease digestive problems, as well as helping the body to detox. They are also a great source of vitamin C and K, and contain small amounts of potassium, calcium, and iron too.

PEAS contain lots of phytonutrients with antioxidant and anti-inflammatory benefits, including some which are exclusively found in these little green gems. They also contain Omega-3 fats in the form of ALAs, and plenty of vitamin E and beta-carotene for healthy skin and eyes.

PECANS are lovely and buttery in baking and are a great source of energy. They are rich in fatty acids and also contain vitamin E to rid the body of toxic free radicals and protect from diseases.

PINEAPPLE has been used for centuries to treat digestive problems and inflammation. It's high in antioxidants such as vitamins C, beta-carotene, and the minerals copper, zinc, and folate.

PINE NUTS are naturally sweet and delicious, but are also a good source of plant-derived nutrients, vitamins, and minerals, as well as heart-healthy monounsaturated fatty acids. Their high vitamin E content makes them great for the skin.

POMEGRANATES are like nature's rubies—they just look so beautiful when added to dishes. This nutrient-dense and antioxidant-rich fruit (the most powerful of all the fruits) is also an ancient symbol of fertility and health.

POTATOES can have quite a bad reputation, with most people in health and fitness circles avoiding them. However, they can help to fight inflammation and are even known to lower blood pressure. They're also rich in vitamin B6, which can build cells and support the body's nervous system.

PUMPKIN SEEDS are a tasty source of vitamin B and iron.

QUINOA, actually a pseudo-cereal, is a great option for anyone with a gluten intolerance, and is one of my favorite healthy carbs. It's a brilliant source of protein, fatty acids, as well as B vitamins, magnesium, and calcium. It is a fiber-rich whole grain, and so wonderful for digestion.

RAISINS are a wonderful high-energy food that contain high levels of the antioxidant catechin.

RASPBERRIES are lower in sugar than many fruits but also provide you with plenty of vitamin C and other antioxidants. They are also high in flavonoids.

RHUBARB is full of nutrients. Tart and sweet, the stalks are high in vitamin K, which we need for

bone health and strengthening, and minerals such as iron, copper, calcium, potassium, and phosphorus. They also contain certain compounds which transform into vitamin A inside the body—a powerful natural antioxidant which helps to keep the skin healthy and fresh.

ROSEMARY is great at improving digestion and is full of anti-inflammatory and antioxidant compounds.

SAFFRON is one of the world's most highly prized spices and is loved for its color, intense flavor, and medicinal properties. It's high in plant-based chemical compounds that have antioxidant and disease-preventing qualities, while it also has therapeutic uses as an antiseptic and anti-depressant. It's also been used for treating everyday problems, including asthma, coughs and colds, insomnia, PMT, and heartburn.

SAGE offers an array of health benefits. Its rosmarinic acid can act as both an anti-inflammatory and antioxidant and is even thought to enhance memory.

SALMON is packed full of goodness and body-loving properties. It's high in Omega-3s and is also a good source of skin-boosting vitamin E. It's also a wonderful source of lean protein for muscle building and repair, and also contains essential amino acids and vitamins A, D, B6, and B.

SESAME OIL and **SESAME SEEDS** are packed with magnesium as well as zinc, which is essential for producing collagen to smooth out wrinkles and plump up the skin. Sesame is also one of the best sources of calcium on the planet. **Tahini**, a paste made from sesame seeds, is one of my favorite ingredients and I love to add it to dressings and sauces for an added health boost.

SHALLOTS generally have a higher mineral content than your typical onion. They are also high in antioxidants, which are released when the shallot is crushed or sliced, and contain iron to boost energy, cell regrowth, healing, and metabolism.

SMOKED HADDOCK is a fantastic source of lean protein, so is great for keeping you full and satisfied. It's also loaded with minerals, including magnesium, potassium, iron, calcium, and selenium. Be sure to buy your smoked haddock free from the yellow food dye often added to make it look more attractive.

SHRIMP are a fantastic source of protein, and good at boosting our Omega-3 levels.

SOFT BROWN SUGAR has a really distinctive taste and is less heavily processed and refined than your standard white table sugar. Thanks to this, it retains all of the nutrients you find in cane sugar —minerals such as potassium, calcium, and iron.

SPINACH is one of those leafy greens that just keeps on giving, full of body-loving boosters. I like to add handfuls to all sorts of meals—including green smoothies —since it is so high in vitamin C and full of anti-inflammatories and antioxidants. Adding spinach to your diet is also a great way to dose up on vitamin K, which is good for strong bones. It's also a wonderful source of energy, contains folic acid, and can improve the quality of the blood, thanks to its high iron content.

SQUID adds a lean form of protein to your diet, and are

extremely high in copper, which is essential for helping the body to absorb iron.

STEVIA is a natural sugar substitute, and is about three times as sweet as ordinary sugars.

SUNFLOWER SEEDS are a good way to get folate in pregnancy.

SWEET POTATOES are one of the healthiest foods on the planet. They're an excellent source of vitamin C and are also rich in vitamin D, which boosts the immune system, helps to raise energy levels, and can even make us feel happier. Their high vitamin E content is good for fresh, youthful skin, and their beta-carotene is antioxidant and antiviral.

TARRAGON contains plenty of phytonutrients, antioxidants and vitamin C to help boost health and prevent disease. The compounds found in this delicious herb are also known to stimulate appetite.

THYME is a good source of vitamins C and A, iron, manganese, copper, and dietary fiber. It's also believed to fight bacteria found in foods.

TOFU is an ideal vegan source of protein as it contains all eight essential amino acids. It is also high in iron and calcium, as well as manganese, selenium, phosphorous, magnesium, and zinc.

TOMATOES are incredibly nutrient-dense and contain an array of nutrients and antioxidants, including alpha-lipoic acid, which helps to convert glucose to energy, and lycopene, which helps to protect against free radicals. They are also a good source of vitamins A and C, as well as folic acid, making

them the perfect staple for pregnant women.

TURKEY is very lean and the high levels of protein will keep you full for hours. It also contains selenium.

TURMERIC is a superspice and a traditional remedy for all sorts of ailments, including depression, bloating, jaundice, menstrual pain, toothache, bruises, and even colic in young babies. It contains curcumin, a powerful antioxidant that has strong anti-inflammatory effects to ward off colds and flu.

WALNUTS are packed with Omega-3 fatty acids—great for glowing skin and hair.

ZUCCHINI make healthy living so much easier and more exciting. They are a good source of folates, which are beneficial to the fetus during pregnancy. They're also a great way to get heart-healthy potassium into your diet, which can help to reduce blood pressure.

INDEX

Firstly a huge thank you to my mom, Natalie, and dad, Phil. Without their hard work and dedication, none of this would have been possible. They are the reason I have such a passion for healthy eating. They made growing up a celiac easier and more enjoyable with all the homemade gluten-free dishes they rustled up over the years. I'm sure my sister, Daisy, and brother, Jack, will agree.

The Lucy Bee team all worked so hard together to compile the delicious recipes for this book. It was a group effort and the hard work really did pay off. Petrina Grint—Thank you for being there 24/7. Your organization made a crazy busy time so much easier. I'm so lucky to work with someone who cares so much. Meg Phizacklea—It's always enjoyable working with people you love spending time with. I can't wait for many more fun times ahead. Sam Hadadi—You have a real talent in the kitchen and I'm so thankful that you let us share some of your recipes. Karl Brown, The Trainer—aka Mr. Positive—You bring sunshine on a rainy day! Hannah Grint—Spicing up the timeline on twitter! Thanks for all you do on social media and I'm looking forward to what's to come. Sarah Pearce—Baking at its best. I loved all the recipes you contributed and I'm sure everyone else will too. Ash Buckingham— I enjoyed spending time with you in the kitchen, coming up with mouthwatering recipes on a sunny day! I learned so much. Thanks Uncle Ash! Jim Kinloch and Edward Palmer—Thanks for continuously coming up with new ideas as we move forward. Sorry your Big Boy BBQ Ribs didn't make it in this time! Indra Clementson—Thank you for introducing us to coconut oil so many years ago! I really don't know where we'd be without it.

To Quadrille Publishing, thank you for this incredible opportunity. It's a dream come true! To all the girls who worked so hard to make this book look better than we could ever have imagined. Thank you again for your hard work, music choices and laughter while working together—it was a great time. So thanks to Lisa Pendreigh, Katherine Keeble, Emily Lapworth, Ria Osborne, Hannah Hughes, Emily Jonzen, Jenna Leiter, Poppy Mahon, and Holly Bruce.

Finally, Lucy Bee Lovers—Where would we be without all of you? Due to your consistent loyalty and love for the brand you inspire us every day! Thank you x

LUCY BEE is behind the leading brand of coconut oil in the UK. The product is widely regarded as the best on the market, being raw, organic, extra virgin, cold pressed, and fair trade. Lucy wasdiagnosed as a celiac at 18 months and so her parents instigated healthy lifestyle changes. This included switching to coconut oil seven years ago and they haven't looked back. The lack of availability of a good source in the UK led them to launch their own brand.
www.lucybee.co